anri Woodcarvings

Philly Rains & Donald Bull

Bottle Stoppers
Corkscrews
Nutcrackers
Toothpick Holders
Smoking Accessories
and More

Schiffer® Publishing Ltd
4880 Lower Valley Road, Atglen, PA 19310 USA

Library of Congress Cataloging-in-Publication Data

Rains, Philly.
ANRI woodcarving / Philly Rains & Donald Bull.
p. cm.
1. Anri, s.p.a.--Catalogs. 2. Wood-carving--Collectors and collecting--Italy--Trentino-Alto Adige--Catalogs. I. Bull, Donald. II. Title.
NK9752. A3 T747 2001
730'.92--dc21
2001003206

Designed by Bonnie M. Hensley
Cover design by Bruce M. Waters
Type set in Zapf Chancery Bd BT/Aldine 721 BT

ISBN: 0-7643-1421-1
Printed in China
1 2 3 4

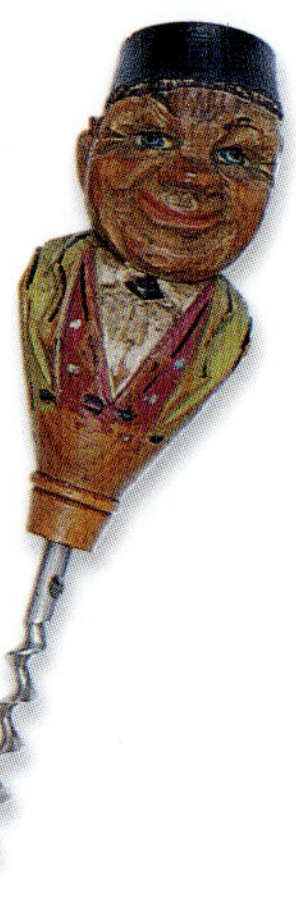

Published by Schiffer Publishing Ltd.
4880 Lower Valley Road
Atglen, PA 19310
Phone: (610) 593-1777; Fax: (610) 593-2002
E-mail: Schifferbk@aol.com
Please visit our web site catalog at **www.schifferbooks.com**
We are always looking for people to write books on new and related subjects. If you have an idea for a book please contact us at the above address.

This book may be purchased from the publisher.
Include $3.95 for shipping.
Please try your bookstore first.
You may write for a free catalog.

In Europe, Schiffer books are distributed by
Bushwood Books
6 Marksbury Ave.
Kew Gardens
Surrey TW9 4JF England
Phone: 44 (0)20-8392-8585
Fax: 44 (0)20-8392-9876
E-mail: Bushwd@aol.com
Free postage in the UK. Europe: air mail at cost

Dedications

To my parents, Beth and Phil Herlein, my son, Scott Williams, his wife Liane, and my precious granddaughter, Aby the Wonderful . . . Philly Rains

To my father, Rev. Major Howard E. Bull
(January 24, 1916-January 16, 2001) . . . Donald Bull

To Anton Riffeser . . . Philly & Don

IN MEMORY OF

Bill Kneisel
August 14, 1946 - March 5, 2001

Foreword

When I heard that Philly Rains and Don Bull were planning to write a book about ANRI, I was very surprised but also curious to see how they would be able to get everything together. In fact, these items were done in many different styles and forms during and between the World Wars, a period which was not the most favorable for our region. ANRI was also involved in creating various utensils and I was very surprised to see how many different pieces they were able to gather.

A very particular aspect of the bottle stoppers was that they were created in the traditional way in the homes during the long winter nights; fathers occupied themselves with the carving while women were busy painting. When the end of the month arrived and the families had to deliver their hard work to the merchants, they also had to expect surprises. The better they did their work the more they got paid and they were especially rewarded for all the tricky moving parts, but often they had to deal with the breakage problem. For that reason, there were specialists in this "cottage industry." Unfortunately, nowadays there is nobody left devoting his time to these souvenirs, which must have a low price in order to be sold.

I am sure that a good part of the collection illustrated in this book is composed of unique pieces, principally because they were all entirely and minutely hand carved, therefore not one bottle stopper looked like the other. From the different styles, we were able to tell their source.

And now I would like to tell you a short anecdote:

When I started to manage the ANRI workshops, and the bottle stoppers were not as popular as before, one lady called *Anda Maria da Ruacia* came personally to my office. She carried a shoebox full of bottle stoppers and offered them to me. I tried to explain to her that due to a decrease in demand we had difficulties in selling them. She was not happy with my answer. *Anda Maria da Ruacia* explained that when she delivered her first bottle stoppers to my grandmother back in the late 1920s, she promised to buy all her lifetime production, if the quality remained the same. The bottle stoppers contained in the box were exactly as they used to be in the past, with the same characteristics. So, I was privileged to buy her beautiful artwork and *Anda Maria da Ruacia* was pleased to have sold the whole content of her shoebox, which was "her last production," as she said.

Now, for all those interested in this book, I am certain that Philly and Don have done an exceptional work to get all the details of this product but I am sure that there are others around, keep an eye open!

Best personal regards

Ernst Riffeser
President
ANRI

Contents

Acknowledgments

First, we would like to thank Ernst and Thomas Riffeser, and the staff at ANRI, for their tireless assistance with this book. No question was too trivial, and no detail was too obscure for their research efforts, and we couldn't have done it without them.

We would also like to thank some very special collectors who contributed precious items from their own collections for inclusion among these pages; Jack and Betty Bandy, Punky and Jeff Barrett, Dot and Don Enockson, Joe Iozzia, Pat Jordan, Bill Kneisel, Dee Konyha, Ron MacLean, Ken Schnoll, Mike Sharp, Hondo Swedlund, and Sue Theurich. While some of them have been our personal friends for many years, others are friends we have yet to actually meet face to face. We hope to remedy that someday.

Philly Rains and Don Bull

. . . and a personal note from Philly:

Thanks to my family for allowing me the time and space to work on this project, even as I neglected them in the process. Thank you for not whining, and for your loyal support. I hope you'll be proud of this accomplishment.

. . . and a personal note from Don:

Thank you to my wife, Bonnie, for collecting ANRI items with me and sharing thoughts and time for this book.

Introduction

The History of ANRI

The home of ANRI sits in the lovely village of St. Christina high in the Gröden Valley, the Italian Val Gardena. Long before there were paved roads or even railways, the Gröden Valley was home to hundreds of woodcarvers who made the hard trek across dangerous mountain passes to sell their wares to the European markets.

Alois Riffeser, the son of an established wood carver and trader, was born in St. Christina in 1854. At the age of twelve he was sent abroad to sell the family's woodcarvings, but was soon brought home when his father died suddenly. Alois was an active merchant who continued to sell his carvings to foreign markets.

The first Anton Riffeser was Alois' son, born in 1887. Anton carried on his family's tradition and founded the ANRI Company which he named using the first two letters of his first and last names. He was married in 1912 to Karoline and soon their son, Anton Jr., was born.

When World War I broke out, Anton Riffeser was a 27-year-old father, but his sense of duty compelled him to join the Austrian Emperor's Tyrolean Guard regiment and he was sent to the Russian front with a group of his fellow Grödeners. They were soon captured by the enemy and sent to a prisoner of war camp in Siberia. During that first winter 2,000 men died.

Anton and his friends survived. They lived and worked together in the camp, where they continued to practice their carving skills, often using the local Russian peasants as models. It was while Anton was held prisoner for five long years that he formulated his plan for a woodcarving company he would call ANRI. It was also during this time that he learned to speak English. When the war ended and he and his fellow carvers returned to the Gröden Valley in 1920, he was ready to begin an international business.

Although they were shocked to discover that the South Tyrol region had been ceded to Italy, they soon recovered and began producing carvings again. In 1926, Anton Riffeser Sr., constructed a new building in St. Christina, which housed his family, workshops, a warehouse, and offices. Anton Jr., now 14, joined his parents in the family business. Over 100 families were involved in the production of early ANRI products. The European markets were flourishing once again and for the first time ANRI carvings were introduced in the United States. During the long winter months, when travel was impossible, some men and women carved and painted in their own homes. In the spring, their creations were collected for sale around the world. Others worked in ANRI's workshops or in their own studios.

War broke out again thirteen years later and business was halted. When the war ended in 1945, production was resumed and soon the ANRI company employed 500 families in the Gröden Valley. Anton felt that it was important to control the quality and consistency of the carvings, so in 1950 he built new workshops with better lighting and improved working conditions. ANRI agencies were opened all over the world.

Anton Sr. died in 1969. The next year Anton Jr.'s son, Ernst, at the age of 27, took over leadership of the company with the continued support of his father. During the next three decades the business continued to grow along with the collectibles market. Limited Edition carvings designed by Juan Ferrandiz, Sarah Kay, Gunther Granget, Helmut Diller, and others, were being introduced, along with nativity sets designed by Prof. Karl Kuolt, Ulrich Bernardi, J. Bachlechner, and W. Bacher.

When Anton Riffeser, Jr., died in 1982, another Riffeser had entered into the family business, Ernst's son, Thomas. In the early 1990s, Ernst passed the leadership of ANRI to his son, who serves as Director of the Board. For almost 90 years and five generations, ANRI has proudly preserved the art of woodcarving, and still maintains an apprentice system where master woodcarvers, artists, and craftsmen teach their skills to a new generation.

This Book

This book came about because Philly's mailbox and computer inbox were constantly filled with the question, "Where can I find a book on vintage ANRI?" The next question was always, "Then why don't *you* write one?" Philly was reluctant for two reasons. She didn't want to create a price guide that might be perceived as "he with the most stuff sets the values for fun and profit."

The second reason was that once a book is written, the chance of finding something truly unique, at a bargain price, decreases drastically. Everyone dreaded the day when a neat bottle stopper couldn't be bought for less than $20. When Internet antique shops and auctions sites expanded the hunting grounds to encompass the whole world at the push of a button, the dreaded day arrived. The number of collectors seeking information increased and finally, Philly and Don began this labor of love.

It wasn't always easy to decide how to categorize the parts and chapters so there are musicians in the animals section, bottle stoppers among the corkscrews, and some items are where they are simply because it seemed a logical place at the time.

Values

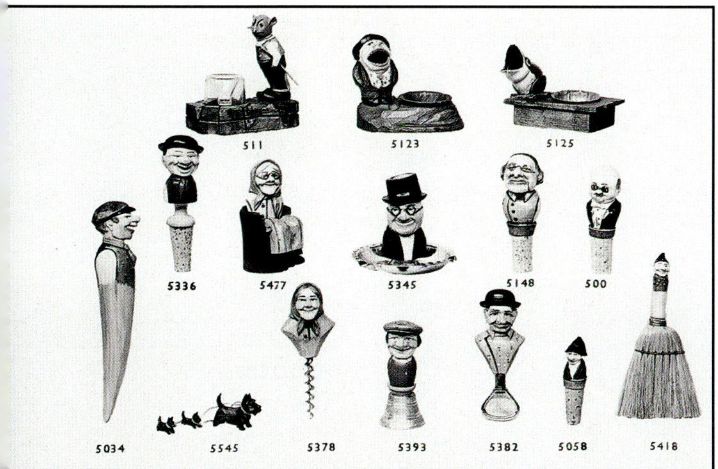

HAND COLOURED & CARVED WOOD

Here is an interesting range of useful articles :

511	Tooth Pick Holder	64/- per doz.	500	Bottle Cork	18/- " "
5123	Ashtray	45/- " "	5034	Paper Knife	11/6 " "
5125	Frog Ashtray	32/- " "	5545	Dog and two puppies	18/- " "
5336	Bottle Cork	12/- " "	5378	Cork Screw	30/- " "
5477	" "	30/- " "	5393	Table Bell	34/- " "
5345	Ashtray	30/- " "	5382	Bottle Opener	30/- " "
5148	Bottle Cork. (Mouth opens)	28/- " "	5058	" Cork	13/6 " "
			5418	Cloth Whisk	22/6 " "

OCEAN TRADING Co. 40 Orchard Lane, SOUTHAMPTON

PHONE 2579 TELEPHONE "KWICK" SOUTHAMPTON

LONDON SHOWROOM :- 10, Eastcheap, E.C.3 PHONE ROYAL 8897

It was important to maintain a balance between "value" and worth. As Philly has said in news media articles, while one person may assign value to something, only the buyer can assign worth. The value ranges herein are based on public and private sales, prices seen in antique shops and Internet sales, and what is considered the *true* value, based on availability, scarcity, and age. The value ranges given are for items in very good to mint condition and may not apply to the ones photographed.

Factors that decrease value:
- Broken or missing parts
- Inoperable mechanisms
- Poor reconditioning
- Uneducated sellers
- Apathetic sellers

Factors that increase value:
- Buyer competition
- Over zealous buyers
- Low supply and high demand
- Condition of an item
- Original label, mark, or sticker

Please note that the value ranges in this book represent estimates of current selling prices of ANRI carvings in very good condition. Neither the authors nor the publisher will be responsible for any gain or loss experienced by using the value guidelines.

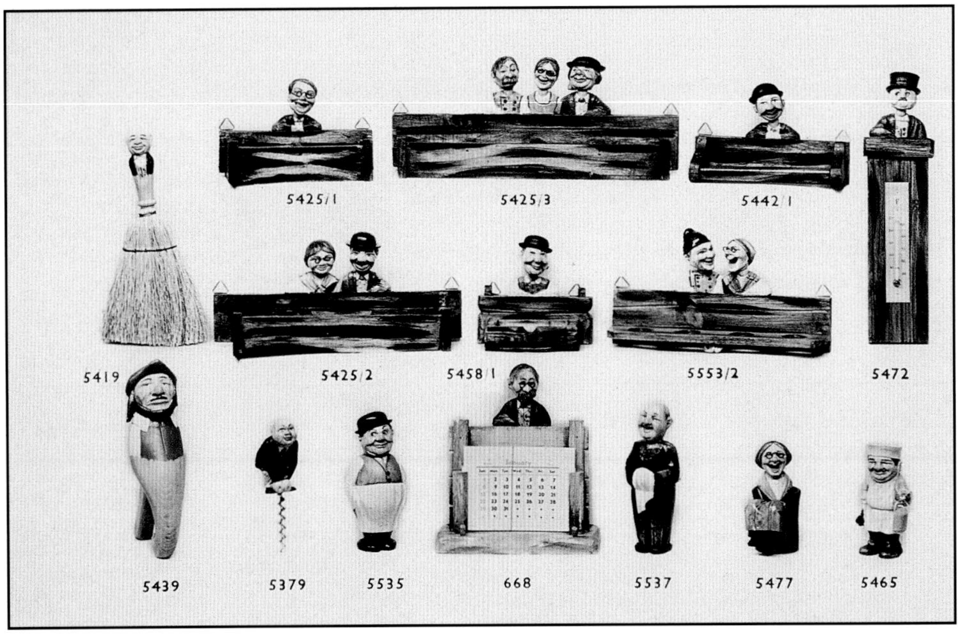

HAND COLOURED & CARVED WOOD

Here is an interesting range of useful articles :

5425/1	Pipe Rack	36/- per doz.	5439	Nut Cracker	32/- " "
5425/3	" "	90/- " "	5379	Bartender with Cork Screw	40/- " "
5442/1	Tie "	34/- " "	5535	Bottle Cork. Standing Figure.	34/- " "
5419	Cloth Whisk	34/- " "	668	Calendar	45/- " "
5425/2	Pipe Rack	66/- " "	5537	Bartender with Bottle Opener	40 - " "
5458/1	" "	36/- " "	5477	Bottle Cork. Sitting Figure	30/- " "
5553/2	" "	56/- " "	5465	Egg Timer	45/- " "
5472	Themometer	52/- " "			

OCEAN TRADING Co. 40 Orchard Lane, SOUTHAMPTON

PHONE 2579 TELEPHONE "KWICK" SOUTHAMPTON

LONDON SHOWROOM :- 10, Eastcheap, E.C.3 PHONE ROYAL 8897

To be Mint, a carving must be completely original with no cracks or chips, have no major paint loss, and function as designed. Replaced parts, obvious reconstruction, or major repairs lower value. For items having them, music boxes should play.

Bottle stoppers with original corks are more appealing but little value is lost for minor breaks and chips in the corks. Chipped hats and noses are natural occurrences. Naturally, as wine flows the drinker's dexterity decreases and bar items get dropped. Bottle stoppers with mechanical parts should function properly. If the stopper is designed to rest in one position, it should return to that position after the string is pulled, lever depressed, or peg twisted.

Most ANRI stoppers originally had tapered corks extending 1 ½" below their wooden bases. Some had "Italy" stamped in ink on the bottom or side of the cork. On others, ANRI labels were applied. The corks originally used by the ANRI Company are no longer available, which brings us to the subject of what to do about broken corks.

Buying stoppers with replacement corks is a matter of individual choice. A few battle chips are preferable to bad repairs. A stopper with an old wine cork glued to it for good appearance is OK. However, collectors should be aware that new corks are being altered and "aged" with tea or coffee to replicate the originals. To protect your investment, ask questions. An honest seller will inform you of any known "improvements." If you plan on reselling your own collection, avoid repainting or even doing touch ups which lower value.

Dating Key and Guidelines

When attempting to determine the age of ANRI carvings, there are few guidelines but many pitfalls. If the item still has a label, you can compare it to the dating key. Unfortunately, early ANRI labels were small and many were removed or fell off years ago. The ANRI sticker in 1925 was black and white, 5/16" diameter. The brown and cream-colored label, 3/8" diameter was used continuously from 1926 through 1950, consequently dating items during that period is especially difficult. The green and gold foil pine tree label used from 1954 through 1967 is the one most commonly found.

Catalogs are helpful as visual references but collectors should not rely on catalog numbers or item titles. ANRI assigned titles to only a few items in the early years but as they began to enter the "collectibles" market, item titles became a more frequent practice. It has been problematic for collectors that the titles sometimes changed from one year, or from one catalog, to the next. This is especially true of figurines produced in the late 1960s.

Measurements in older catalogs were given in both centimeters and inches, but because of the nature of individual carvings and carvers, two items of the same type may differ in size to some degree. For this reason, sizes given on the items in this book apply only to those pictured. The same or similar item in your own collection may be slightly larger or smaller.

Collectors often wonder about the number of elf or gnome carvings ANRI produced. The inspiration for them can be traced to a legend that is still being told today.

Grödeners say that many years ago, a young shepherd boy was searching for a stray lamb in the mountains when he discovered a cave inhabited by dwarfs. Hiding from view, he saw that they were carving wonderful figures from tiny blocks of wood. When he was discovered and brought to the King of the Dwarfs, the boy asked, "By what magic are these figures produced?" The King told him that it was not magic at all, but that patience and skill were the only magic required. "I will teach you, myself!" When the boy returned to the valley he taught others to carve, and in turn they taught their children, and so on for generations to come. ANRI "dwarf" figures were produced in homage to the gift of woodcarving given to the people of the valley long years ago.

Modern collectors call these figures by different names: elves, gnomes, or even sprites. For the sake of simplicity we have chosen to call them gnomes throughout this book. Of course, you may call them whatever you prefer.

There is one other important thing to note about ANRI carvings and how they are produced. Master carvers design and produce an original model. Once a model is approved, many different carvers are employed to make *reproductions* of the original. Therefore, only the design is credited to a specific Master carver. All original Master carvings are kept in the ANRI company archives.

Master Carvers

Eduard Mahlknecht was born in 1897 in St. Ulrich in Gröden. For five years he attended the Professional School at St. Christina/Wolkenstein. In 1923 he began as a model cutter and designer for the ANRI firm under Anton Riffeser where he continued for over 40 years. Most of his designs were for bottle stoppers and bar accessories.

Guilio Sestini was born in 1905 in Livorno. He received his diploma from the Imperial School of Ceramics at Sesto Fiorentino and the Art School of Florence. He began to work exclusively for ANRI in 1950 in the area of new models specializing in music boxes for children, among other items. Sestini, the father in law of Master Carver Ulrich Bernardi, retired from ANRI in 1966.

Siegfreid Hafner, was born in 1925, a native of Lienz, Tyrol, and settled in Innsbruck after graduating from the Academy of Arts in Vienna. ANRI carried a line of Hafner carvings depicting whimsical children from the 1960s to early 1970s.

Josef Malfertheiner was born in 1931 in St. Ulrich in Northern Italy's Gröden Valley and attended the local Academy of Art. After a stint in the Military he opened his own workshop and began a long-standing relationship with ANRI. As a master carver, he was known for his extraordinary series of bas-reliefs depicting scenes from Tyrolean history, and representations of the works of Rembrandt, Van Eyck, Renoir, Spitzweg, and others.

Contacts

If you have comments or questions about this book, please write the authors at:

Philly Rains
1401 Brentwood Drive
Harrison, AR 72601
email: philly@anricarvings.com
Website: www.anricarvings.com

or

Donald Bull
P. O. Box 596
Wirtz, VA 24184
email: corkscrew@bullworks.net
Website: http://www.corkscrewmuseum.com

Part One

ANRI for the Desk

When the ANRI Company was formed in 1912, it is doubtful anyone imagined that the very items being carved and painted then would survive to delight and amaze us almost 90 years later. But, survive they have and in astounding numbers.

What is perhaps even more awe inspiring is that these carvings from the earliest years are still beautiful, still functional, and in many cases, are more highly valued now than on the day they were created.

ANRI carvings were produced to brighten the home and help with daily tasks. While some of those tasks have changed over the years, there is hardly a single item in this book that is no longer useful and able to accomplish that for which it was originally intended. And there is no better definition for *enduring quality* than that.

Desk Accessories

When we consider desks, whether in an office or at home, there are some things we use every day that are necessary parts of our lives. We wouldn't function as well without them. Bookends, calendars, paper clips, pens, letter openers, and bookmarks fall into this category.

In this chapter we discover that while the need for these items hasn't diminished, perhaps similar items produced today have lost the beauty and character they once held when ANRI made desk accessories.

Another pair of bookends shown in the 1921 ANRI catalog has a gnome with a concertina matched with another sitting on a rock, peacefully smoking a pipe. The set pictured here featuring two musicians and the set above, are excellent examples of the creativity and attention to detail that make ANRI creations so desirable today. 5 7/8" tall, 3 5/8" wide, and 3 5/8" deep. $200-225.

A pair of bookends pictured in a 1921 ANRI catalog look very much like these featuring a mountain climbing gnome and his companion playing a mandolin. In catalog illustrations from 1925 and 1926 the gnome bookend designs had expanded to five with gnomes shown playing flutes, drums, bass fiddles, and a horn resembling a saxophone. 5" tall, 3.5" wide, and 4" deep. $200-250.

Bookends carved with Gröden Valley citizens and musical instruments were also produced, and although minor details vary from set to set, the characters remain familiar. This pair, introduced in the 1926 catalogs, remained in production into the mid-1960s. 5" wide by 4" deep, and 4" tall. $200-225.

The bookends seen here were not produced as a matching set, but are orphan bookends from pairs that have become separated from their mates over the years. Notice the difference in style and carving on each base. Single Bookend, $75-100.

ANRI added this pair of monks with musical instruments in the late 1920s and the design remained consistent throughout its production into the 1960s. 5.5" tall, 3.5" wide, 4" deep. $175-200.

In the early 1920s the carvers of ANRI began producing this set with a man and woman seated in red wing back chairs turning to see each other. Production continued well into the 1960s. The first sets were about 3" wide, and 6" to 6.5" tall. In the final years the set had grown to 9" tall, and over 6" wide to accommodate larger modern books. A collectors' favorite then, as now, almost 80 years later. Early sets, $250-275. Larger sets, $100-150.

ANRI produced bookends featuring dogs before 1921 and by the late 1920s had added bears, elephants, lions, fawns, and small 'scenes' with gnomes, pine trees, and forest creatures. This set features a Scottish terrier on one side and a wire-haired fox terrier on the other. They are 6" long by 8" tall, and 4" wide at the base. The highly detailed heads measure 4.5" to 5" from nose to tips of ears, and 3.5" to 4.5" wide. $175-200.

This pair with a Pekinese and a Schnauzer stands 5" tall, 3.75" wide, and 4" to 5" deep. On the bottom, along with the original thin layer of felt paper for protecting furniture, is an ANRI label from 1925. Along the edge of the bookend with the Pekinese, are the words, "Ste. Anne de Beaupre." $175-200.

Another pair of friendly canines has the taller backboard for larger books. They are 6" tall, 3.5" long, and 4" wide. The figures of a Skye terrier and a Saint Bernard stand 3.25" to 4" tall. Other styles were made with picket fences having dogs standing on their hind legs. Many breeds were sold in combination. Some dogs were carved lying down and others sitting with one paw up. $150-175.

Two figures in the typical dress of the people of the Tyrol are shown doing daily tasks. The man bookend is 7.75" tall, 4" wide, and 4" deep. The lady is only 7" tall. $150-175.

From the mid-1950s, and continuing into the 1960s, ANRI produced a series of busts honoring famous writers and composers. Some models contained music boxes, while others were produced as bookends. They are identified by the names made of brass inserted into the bases such as the Beethoven and Dante busts shown here. It is important to note that the heads themselves were made of a composite substance called Sculptulite under the ANRI "Toriart" label, but the bases are wood. $50-75.

This single bookend has a lady caricature looking out a window. Slightly over 7" tall, 4.75" wide, and 1.5" deep. $40-55.

No desk was complete without a calendar and these guaranteed a smile each day. They are "perpetual calendars" which use a system of printed cards to mark the date. This requires 3 cards for the months, seven "month at a glance" cards, and two cards for the days of the week. ANRI was producing only a few calendars of this type by the end of the 1960s.

The two ANRI desk calendars shown here are 6.5" wide, 2.5" deep, and 6.75" to 7" tall. At the base of some models a "pen rest" is provided. The pen seen here is another ANRI creation that was sold without the metal nib. Calendar with complete card set, $115-125.

This calendar has the cards removed to better show the wooden pegs for holding a pen. All calendar figures have the neck/bead feature allowing the heads to turn. To be considered "mint," the heads must be movable. Calendars without cards, $65-85.

Smaller models were made without the pen rest feature. From the left a man in native attire, a Skye terrier, and a man in side view are shown. The man on the right has had a slight mishap in the area just above his mouth, but his calendar is always right on the nose. These calendars measures 4" to 4.5" wide, 1.25" to 1.75" deep, and 4" to 4.75" tall. $75-90.

This exceptional desk calendar also includes a handy thermometer and a nice wide pen rest at the front of the base. The thermometer no longer functions, but the calendar always will. Notice that the card set has the 1926 ANRI logo printed on the front, as well as on every card in this complete set. 8" wide, 3.5" deep, and 6" tall at the roof above the thermometer. $125-150.

These are ANRI perpetual wall calendars that use a system of ribbons to display the day and date as viewed through "windows" cut into the wood. Notice that only one set of ribbons is printed in English. The Alpine children have the neck/bead movable heads. The small kitchen vignettes were also produced without the calendar feature and sold separately. $65-80.

During the 1950s and early 1960s, a new line of figures was designed by Cristi, including sportsmen, doctors, musicians, and other professionals. Cristi figures were sold separately, and attached to desk clocks and barometers. In a late 1950s trade catalog, ANRI stated that the clocks and barometers were manufactured in Germany and fully guaranteed. The two Cristi models shown are a doctor and a golf caddy that retains the gold and green pine tree label ANRI used from 1954 through 1967. 7" tall by 7" wide. $95-125.

Paper clips haven't always been little pieces of twisted metal. ANRI produced paper clips or clamps that were carved with happy Gröden Valley faces, designed to sit atop a desk or hang on a wall. 5" long with a metal spring. $100-120.

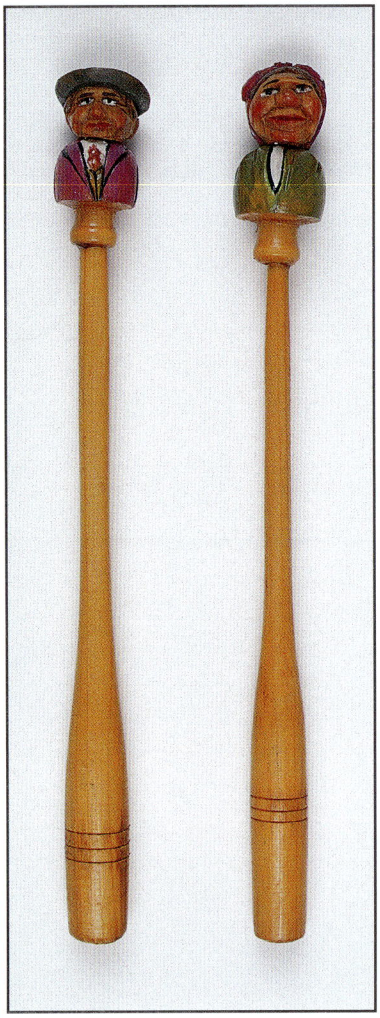

Before the days of ballpoint and fountain pens, people used dip pens for writing. Metal tips, called nibs, were bought separately and inserted into holders made of wood, plastic, and other materials. ANRI pens were pictured in trade catalogs during the 1920s and featured people, dogs, and birds. 5"–6.5" long. $45-75.

Years ago books were sometimes bound leaving the pages folded at the outer edges. The reader used a "paper knife" to cut through the folds and separate the pages. A similar tool was the letter opener, although these were usually much shorter. ANRI produced literally hundreds of both items, but the examples shown here are paper knives. Paper knives may be as long as 14" depending on the figural carving at the handle, but on average measure 12" long. These were carved to closely resemble utility knives with metal blades. Due to age and use, many have broken tips. $65-85.

It's easy to see what made ANRI paper knives so popular. The figures represented here are obviously caricatures, but done with such skill they seem almost lifelike. $65-85.

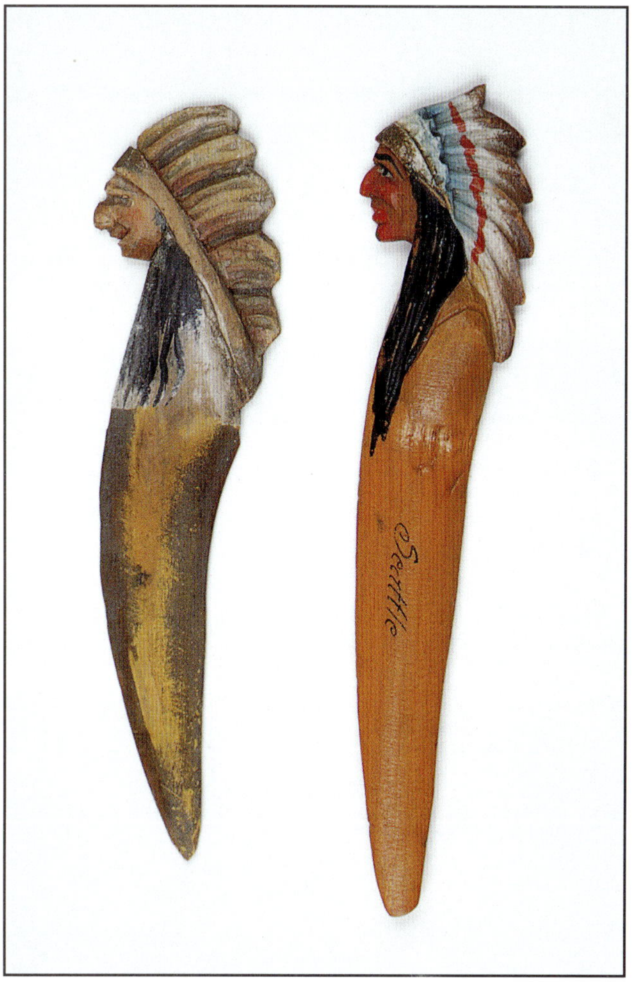

Images of American Indians were not only used in the United States, but also in Europe. They may be found on many ANRI items like letter openers and paper knives. The Indian Chief at left has "Grand Canyon Ariz." hand painted along the blade indicating that it was exported and sold as a souvenir in the United States. Lengths range from 8" to 12". $60-90.

Some letter openers feature animals not indigenous to Europe like the knife topped with a polar bear standing on an iceberg. The ANRI carvers most often used familiar animals like the squirrel climbing a tree. The letter opener with a handle carved like an ear of corn is truly unique. Painted along the blade is "Natl. Corn Husking Contest, Nov. 14, 1930 Norton Kan." Was this a souvenir or the prize? $65-95.

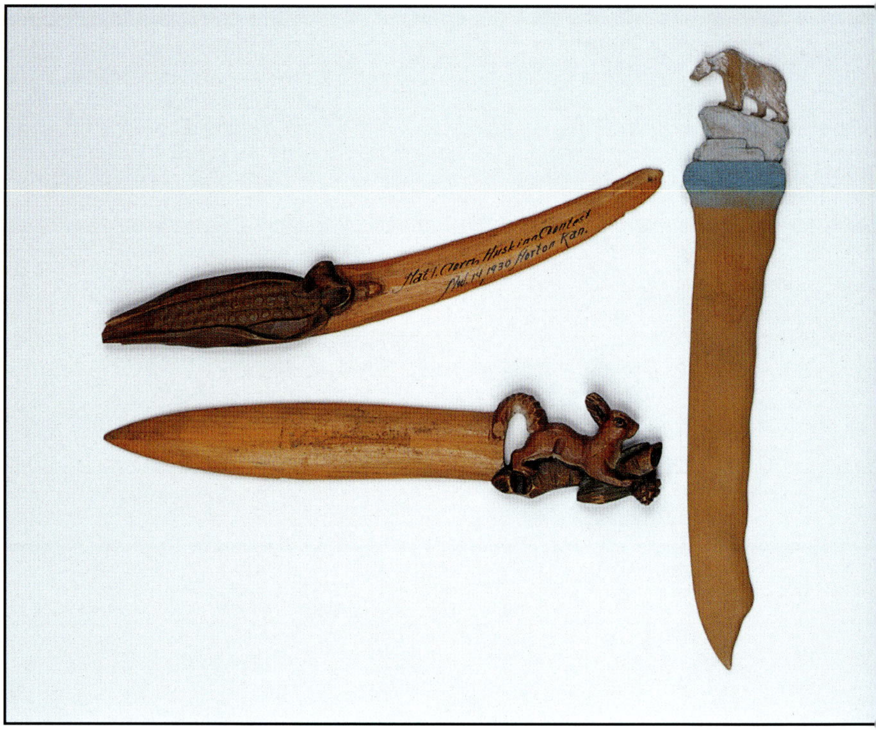

Not all vintage ANRI letter openers have aged well, as witnessed by the two on the left, but others like the Canadian Mounted policeman, gnome, and old man with a pig, are as bright as the day they were carved. The man on the right has a point-protecting stand. $55-75.

The large paper knife on the bottom is 15" long, while the Scottish terrier, man in Derby hat, gnome, and Indian are 8" long. $55-75.

These photos should give collectors a good idea of the variety of caricatures that were produced. An ANRI catalog from 1926 noted that "more than 100 subjects" were available. One is hand lettered on the blade "Ste. Anne de Beaupre," which also appears on a pair of bookends in this chapter. $65-85.

Even small letter openers were carved with great attention to detail. 5" to 6" long. $45-70.

A group of five letter openers ranging from 6" to 10" long plus an 11" paper knife. $40-70.

Small letter openers. 4.5" to 5" long. $40-70.

ANRI bookmarks have a "v" shaped notch cut into the pointed wooden shaft that allows a reader to slip it between pages of a book. The style is not much different than bookmarks made today, but these are generally more interesting. Collectors should look for another style showing figures carved to about mid-thigh, with a notch cut between the blade and the figure's arm. 3" to 4.5". $35-65.

A well-carved group of bookmarks. 3" to 4.5". $35-65.

More small book-marks, but most lack the skill seen in previous examples. $30-60.

ANRI for the Smoker

Smoking accessories adorn many desks. Ashtrays, pipe rests, humidors, and lighters are still seen today, but other things once common have disappeared including match holders, match safes, cigarette boxes, and cigarette holders. ANRI produced accessories for smokers through the early 1970s, but with many fewer items in the line than those produced in the early 1900s. As production of all smoking accessories ended only a few styles of pipe rests, cigarette boxes, and ashtrays were being made.

One of the more familiar cigarette boxes produced by ANRI is a man draped over a barrel. When his coattail is pressed, the barrel opens revealing the cigarettes inside. There are many variations in facial features and hats, but the basic clothing style is consistently a coat with long tails. Most have a cigar or cigarette in the mouths. The barrels measure from 3.75" to 4" tall. Overall, figures can measure 7" tall. To be considered mint, the head should turn freely on the bead/neck, but little value is lost if the head has been made stationary by repair. $55-75.

Some of the "man and barrel" boxes are musical. The one on the left has a suitcase that contains a wind up, Swiss music box that plays "Tennessee Waltz." The one on the right has the music box hidden in the bottom of the barrel. The winder isn't visible without turning the piece upside down. These are usually taller, measuring up to 8". With music, $65-85.

Some figures on this type of box are clowns which are not as plentiful, but fun to find and add to an ANRI collection. $65-85.

Here is another nice group which includes a clown and, in the center, an unusual red barrel. Colored barrels are not as common as the natural colored ones, but do not affect the value of the boxes. The example on the right is an especially nice one with a well-carved face and cigar. $65-85.

The kissing couple cigarette box has a clever design. Pressing a lever at the back of the couple causes the figures to turn and kiss as the top of the box opens. The skill of the carving on the figures varies from piece to piece. Compare the faces on the right with the other two and you can see which is the more attractive and desirable. Cigarette boxes are 4" square and overall height varies up to 6.5" tall. ANRI cigarette boxes of this type were designed for small, unfiltered cigarettes. $65-90.

Cigarette boxes with dog breeds are another charming ANRI item. To the left is a Scottish terrier and on the right, a wirehaired fox terrier. Pressing down on the dogs' tails lifts the tops. Boxes measure 4.25" by 3.5". Many dog breeds may be found. Beware of similar "knock offs" produced in Japan. Some may not be marked so it is important to study the way in which the genuine carvings were crafted. $100-125.

This style includes both a dog and a tormented cat. The boxes have a peaked roof to represent "dog houses" and sit atop a base to which the dogs are attached. The base measures 5.75" by 4". Dog breeds vary as do the colors of the cats. Pressing down on the dogs' tails lifts the lid. $100-130.

Here are two more dog boxes with a yellow and white cat on the left. Both dogs are Skye terriers. $100-130.

One of the most clever and well-done cigarette boxes in the ANRI line is a man on top of a packing crate. When tilted backward, he performs a somersault and the lid that is attached to his feet lifts away. At the same time, a music box inside begins to play. When returned to the original position the music box stops. This particular box has the 40th Anniversary ANRI label, 1912-1952, and plays "The Café Mozart." 5.5" by 3.75", and 6.5" tall. Mint condition. $175.

This is a beautiful cigarette box with a carved figure in a red tasseled hat. Behind his left shoulder is a button/plunger that when pressed, presents a cigarette through his mouth. The box is 8" tall at the man's head, 5" wide and 4.75" deep. $225.

Figural cigarette boxes like these enchanting creations are difficult to find. Produced during the 1920s through 1940s, they feature many styles of clothing and a variety of faces. The hat lifts off and cigarettes are stored inside the hollow body. 5" to 6" tall. The figure on the left may be a caricature of Oliver Hardy, a popular screen star of the era. $150-175.

This pair features a man in a round brimless cap and another in a floppy knit cap with a tassel. The figure on the right is smoking a pipe. $150-175

Not all ANRI boxes of this type are found with their hat/tops intact. A monk is seen on the left and the other three are typical Tyrolean figures. To date, no women figures have been found. These range from 5" to 6". Without tops, $90-120.

In ANRI catalogs from the mid-1920s similar cigarette boxes are pictured featuring breeds of dogs. This Pekinese is 5.5" tall and has part of a 1925 label under the base. Other breeds were produced including Spaniels and Skye terriers. $175-190.

This model from the mid-1920s depicts a basket of dogs and was made in two sizes. The first one has an adult dog and one pup and the second one has two puppies. The smaller box is 6" tall and the other is over 7" tall. Skye terrier carvings may be painted in shades of brown, gray, or white. $185-200.

This cigarette box is much more elaborate with a large wooden dome atop a wood base. The Skye terrier is attached to the dome at the front paws and when the tail is depressed, the box opens. Springs hidden beneath the back paws automatically close the dome when the tail is released. The base is 5.5" by over 3", the bowl is over 3.25" diameter, and the box is over 6" tall, overall. Both the base and bowl are walnut. Mint. $225.

ANRI's most impressive smoking accessory, in both size and quality of carving, is this tobacco humidor made in the same style as the companion cigarette box. This Skye terrier stands over 11" tall on a 10" by 6" base. The bowl is 5.25" diameter and both the bowl and base are made of walnut.

The dog figure has an open, deeply carved mouth with an articulated tongue and teeth. Depressing the tail opens the dome and springs beneath the back paws close the top automatically when the tail is released. An illustration of this humidor is shown in an ANRI trade catalog from 1926. The one shown here is in mint condition. $500.

ANRI made hundreds of small cup-like vessels for holding matches or toothpicks. It is almost impossible to know which is which, so that they have become practically interchangeable. If a small piece of sandpaper or scratching surface is attached to the bottom of a cup, it was meant to hold matches like the two shown here. From 2" to 3" tall. $30-40.

Some match or toothpick holders have a full figure carved on to them or a male figure on one side and a female on the other. 3" tall. $30-40.

This little match girl is mounted on a wooden base and carries a wooden match server on her back. The old size "penny box" of matches would fit neatly on the wooden holder, held slightly opened to make it easy to take a match from the box. The piece is 5" tall and has a 1925 ANRI label. $75.

Here are four views of a rare match safe. The two figures are connected with a wooden hinge and unsnap to reveal a pocket for storing matches. 4.25" tall by 2.75" wide, and 1.25" thick. $300.

ANRI made accessories for pipe smokers, too. Pipe rests were never as charming as when these humorous subjects were carved. This model with the big open smile has depressions for resting three pipes. It was first shown in the 1925 catalog but had disappeared by the early 1950s. $155-185.

Here are three more examples of the pipe rest for three pipes. $185-195.

The unusual pipe rest on the left has a three-dimensional figure. The mouth for the pipe stem is not completely carved through the head. The figure with the hockey stick or golf club is carved in a side view. It holds two pipes and their stems rest on opposite ends of the stick or club. $175-195.

Along with figures of men, ANRI produced many pipe rests with dogs like this model with a pipe smoking English bulldog for two pipes. An interesting addition is the tennis racquet under one arm. Perhaps the dogs in Val Gardena were more talented than those today. $185.

These two pipe holders feature men with sports equipment. Judging by the attire, ANRI carvers weren't actually familiar with the kind of clothing golfers wore. It is unlikely golfers ever hit the links wearing a vest, coat, and derby hat. He is 5" long, 3.25" at the front, and 5" tall. On the right, the tennis player in another unlikely hat is slightly taller. Over 5.75". $175-195.

These pipe racks feature men in Tyrolean dress and a golfer. The fences or wall are rests for pipe stems. 3.5" wide, 4.25" long, 4.5" to 5" tall. $175-185.

This whimsical carving has a little gnome carrying a single pipe rest on his back. $165.

Another pipe rest has a figure lying face down with the feet up. ANRI produced this model as early as 1925, and production continued through the mid-1970s with few changes. Many different male figures were carved plus gnomes and dogs. The dogs were playfully posed, head and chest down, tail in the air. All of them have a hollow back in which the pipes rest. 6.5" by 3.25" tall. $125-155.

An unusual combination pipe rest and humidor. A clown with extended arms sits on a base with depressions for two pipes. A matchbook holder suitcase is on the right, and the head lifts off at the pleated collar to reveal a humidor for tobacco. It has an ANRI green and gold foil pine tree label. The base is 6.5" by 4.5" and overall the carving is 6" tall. $250.

One accessory no smoker can do without is an ashtray. ANRI made so many different types of ashtrays an entire chapter could be devoted to them. This large, round wooden base with applied figures and tree trunks, measures 8" diameter. The base wood is walnut. On the left, a hollow tree holds cigarettes and a smaller one on the right is for matches. The focal point is a 'kissing couple' and in the foreground there is a small rabbit. The ash receiver is ceramic. This piece actually has two ANRI stickers, one on top of the other. The top sticker is a green and gold foil, 40 Year Anniversary label, and beneath that is another one printed in Italian. The top label is 1/2 inch larger. $150.

Other ashtrays with kissing couples were made like this one with barrels and a tin insert. $125.

Kissing couple ashtrays have the same working mechanism as the bottle stoppers. When the lever on the back is depressed the man and woman turn toward each other and kiss. $65-85.

Some ANRI ashtrays have carved figures attached to metal ashtrays. The hollow figure holds matches. 3.75" diameter. $100-120.

On the left, a man with match barrel stands on a four-leaf clover shaped base. It is 5.5" to a side and 5.5" tall. On the right a mechanical violinist tilts his head from side to side and draws his bow across the neck of the instrument when a wooden lever is depressed. 5" diameter, 5.5" tall. $100-150.

This model has a large 8" diameter maple base and a 4" tall barrel for holding cigarettes. Two adorable ANRI canines hold the barrel steady with their paws. The dogs are quite large and have inset glass eyes found on many dog carvings. $150.

Dogs on ashtrays were produced in many forms like this Skye terrier on hind legs against a cigarette barrel. Expect to find many variations with dogs in a variety of poses. Some dogs may also be seen smoking pipes. This one is 3.5" by 5.5" and 4.75" tall at the top of the ears. $100-150.

Some ashtrays were simple affairs with no ash receiver insert. The man is hollow to hold matches. The base is oval shaped, 5" by 3.25", and 3" tall overall. $75-85.

This simple set is missing what was probably a barrel for cigarettes or matches. If complete, $85-95.

Just for fun, as you search for additions to your collection, see how many different models of smoking accessories with dogs you can discover. In this photograph you see, from the left, a pipe rest, a small 4.75" diameter ashtray, and a larger pipe rest/ashtray combination with match holder. $85-150.

Occasionally, ANRI collectors find an item that presents a mystery. This exotic "Swami," in turban and fur trimmed robe, has the look of an ANRI pipe rest and there was probably an ash receiver insert originally.

In back, the hair is carved to extend out from the turban and forms a lever that, when pressed, opens the mouth. A spring inside returns it to the closed position when the lever is released. The turban is hollow for holding cigarettes.

With experimentation it was discovered that the mouth was designed to hold a pipe stem. This very unusual model has the ANRI green and gold foil pine tree label. 5.5" wide by 8" long and over 6" tall. $350.

Other single or double figured racks hold two or three pipes. Lengths vary from 4" to 8" or more depending on the number of holes and figures. Racks of this type were also produced to hold spoons, keys, and matches (see Part Two). $75-95.

Not all ANRI pipe accessories were made to stand on desks or tabletops. Some figural models hang on a wall. This model with three skillfully carved figures holds five pipes. $100-135.

ANRI lighters are uncommon but here are three wonderful examples. To the left and right, single figures conceal old-fashioned, cylinder type lighters. The man on the left separates at the waist with the lighter in the base. The monk on the right has the lighter insert concealed in the neck. The lighter is shown removed in the photograph. The center figure is also a lighter in combination with an ashtray. The head contains the lighter insert. 5" to 6" tall. Single figures, $145-165. With ashtray, $185.

These two carvings also have lighter inserts concealed inside the heads. $145-165.

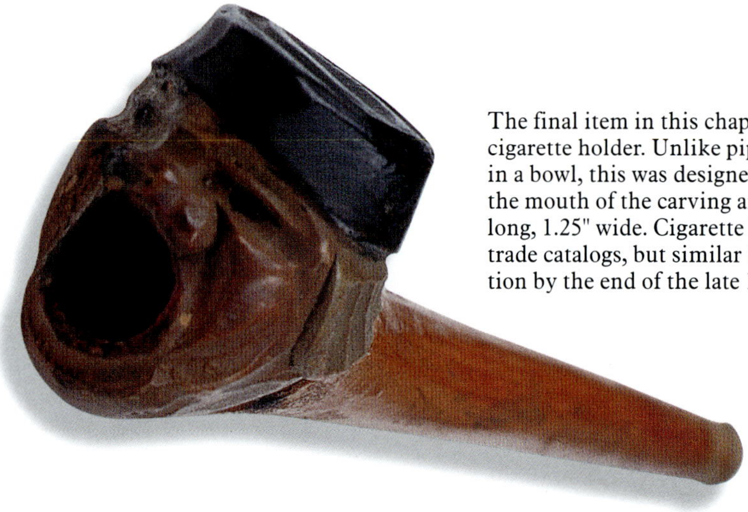

The final item in this chapter on ANRI smoking accessories is a cigarette holder. Unlike pipes, in which loose tobacco is smoked in a bowl, this was designed for a rolled cigarette to be placed into the mouth of the carving and smoked through the stem. It is 4.75" long, 1.25" wide. Cigarette holders were pictured in 1912 ANRI trade catalogs, but similar items had disappeared from production by the end of the late 1920s. $175.

Part Two

ANRI for the Home

From the earliest years, the ANRI product line has pleased the eye and lightened the spirit while serving a useful purpose. In previous chapters we have looked at desk and smoking accessories. Here we examine the hundreds of items made for other places in the home.

Pincushions, decorative boxes, napkin rings, sewing baskets, door knockers, needle cases, toothpick holders, door wedges or door stops, salt and pepper shakers, serving spoons, menu holders, wall hooks, twine boxes, display shelves, figurines, and tiny toys for children, once called "amusements," were pictured in huge numbers in the first catalog ANRI presented in 1912. There was virtually no room in the house that couldn't be enhanced or improved by one of their creations and that's still true today.

ANRI for the Kitchen

When ANRI first began making useful items for the home, a tremendous number of things were designed for use in the kitchen or eating area. The napkin rings, serving spoons and forks, and salt and pepper shakers were an inexpensive way to enliven the family table.

What's for dinner? With an ANRI "menu holder" no one need ask. These sign holders were used for several different purposes, but those pictured in a 1921 ANRI catalog are holding a card that says "Menu." Sadly, they were not pictured in catalogs during 1925 or thereafter. This one is slightly less than 5" tall. $350.

Place card holders are much smaller than menu holders, at 3.5" tall. Carved to resemble the villagers in the Gröden Valley and produced during the 1920s, they, too, had disappeared from ANRI trade catalogs by the early 1950s. $275-300.

Every dining table needs shakers for salt and pepper or a pepper mill. ANRI made many different vessels for dispensing these condiments. Some were sold as sets, but pepper mills could be purchased alone. This matching set of a salt shaker and pepper mill are carved and painted to depict sailors. The pepper mill is 8.75" tall, and the salt shaker is 8". $175.

Both of these are pepper mills but not a matched set. 8 3/8" to 8 5/8" tall. Each, $85.

Small pepper mills were made in this style, as well as in matching sets. These are 3.25" tall and have metal inserts. Peppercorns are ground by turning the knob on top. $75-85.

This group of four shows a pepper mill on the left and three salt containers. The second one from the left is a shaker. The two on the right dispense salt when the wooden buttons on top are depressed. 3.35" to 4" tall. $75-85.

These interesting figures are shakers for either salt or pepper. 4.5" tall. $45-60.

Both of these dainty looking ladies hold salt, which is dispensed when their heads are depressed. The salt is released through the bottom of the base. This model, pictured in an ANRI catalogs from1921, was still being offered through the 1950s and stands 4.5" tall. $55-65.

All of these are shakers with holes in the tops. The pretty lady, second from the left, was probably one of a set, but her mate has been lost. $35-50. The pair on the right is a matching set. The heads remove for filling, 3" tall. Set, $35-45.

Two more matching shaker sets. 3" tall. Set, $35-45.

Another matched set of 3" tall monks. Similar monks were also carved as eggcups. $55-65.

This set of 3.5" tall pigs was introduced in the late 1950s to early 1960s and is one of few figural sets sold with a stand. Others featured carved rabbits, monkeys, and acorns. It measures 5.5" tall to the top of the metal handle. $100-150.

ANRI produced figural serving spoons and forks with "hundreds of subjects" as stated in a trade catalog from 1921. Spoon illustrations included a rooster, an alligator, a stork, a rabbit, a dove, and a lion. Long handled "salad sets" consisting of a fork and spoon with matched figural carvings of a man and woman vary in length from 8" to 11". Per set, $45-75.

These sets illustrate the different clothing styles you may find. $45-60.

Don't be hesitant to add a single fork or spoon to your collection. Wise collectors know that a nice mate may be found eventually. Singles, $25-35.

Due to an unfortunate mix up, two matched sets were inadvertently separated. The middle couple in the first photograph should be mated with the second couple in the next photo. They have since been happily reunited. $45-75.

Hundreds of different models of smaller spoons for serving salt or mustard were made and are still relatively easy to find. Ranging from 3" to 4" long, they were easy to pack and made great souvenirs. Of this group the two on either end lack the carving skill seen in the middle three. $20-35.

Even though "Oberammergau," a German city famous for woodcarvings, is painted on this vintage serving spoon, it was produced by ANRI. This man in a top hat has remnants of a satin fabric shirt collar attached. $100.

Collectors of ANRI should find plenty of different character spoons to keep them interested. $25-40.

Serving paddles and scoops are a little harder to find than spoons. The two on the left are the oldest, produced in the 1920s. Each, $45. Other three shown, $25-30.

Napkin rings have always provided a festive look for the table and the prolific ANRI carvers produced many styles. These feature nodding Alpine children, as found on bottle stoppers and figurines in ANRI trade catalogs. It is important to note that not all napkin rings with these figures were produced by ANRI. Almost identical items with labels from other companies have also been found. $20-30.

If your collection focuses on napkin rings in general, you'll want at least one boy and one girl. They may be found with flowers or musical instruments in hand. $20-35.

Napkin rings similar to these are seen in ANRI trade catalogs beginning in 1925. They have a bead/neck that allows the heads to be turned in any direction and are 3" to 3.5" tall. Many of these have been repaired with glue making the heads immovable. The value of repaired, non-moving napkin rings is only slightly lower than those in original condition. In this style, the body and clothing are carved into the ring and painted in a variety of colors. Instead of wooden beads on each ring, these have tiny shoes to keep them upright. $35-50.

This style has two characters, one on each side. Both have movable bead/necks and are usually found with a man on one side and a woman on the other. As with the single character style in the previous photo, they have carved shoes for stability. $40-55.

Small, full figure carvings were attached to some ANRI napkin rings. This matched pair was produced in the mid-1920s and despite the chip on the man's right foot they make a handsome couple. 4" tall. Matched set, $95.

A wide variety of napkin rings are available for collectors. Even a Canadian Mounted policeman makes an appearance. $25-55.

Another nice group of napkin rings with applied full figured carvings of people. $25-55.

For dog lovers, ANRI applied canines to napkin rings as early as 1926. Trade catalogs from 1921 picture animals carved into the wooden rings, rather than as applied figures. One page shows rams, chamois deer, dogs, rabbits, ducks, cats, and Krazy Kat, a popular cartoon character of the time. 3" to 3.5" tall. $45-65.

The ANRI Skye terrier is second in popularity only to the Scottish terrier and collectors compete for items featuring exclusive breeds. The large napkin ring has the applied dog figurine, and inset glass eyes. $55-65.

No, that's not a napkin ring with two dogs. The one on the left is just visting. $45-65.

One of the more charming napkin ring styles has a movable head with arms that encircle the napkin. Other models have both the man and woman carved onto a single ring. These were pictured in ANRI trade catalogs from 1925 until the 1950s. 3.5" tall. $45-60.

This style of ANRI napkin ring with the characters carved into the ring and extending above the top edge, were shown in every trade catalog from 1921 through 1926, but had disappeared from those printed in the 1950s. $35-50.

A tag on these says they were purchased in 1925. $35-50.

These are similar to the previous three but are carved and painte with greater detai and skill. This style was produce from the late 192(to the mid-1940s. $45-60.

In this style the figures are carved into the napkin ring. $35-50.

It was once common to see eggcups on breakfast tables each morning. Some ANRI eggcups were carved with pedestals, while others, like these monks, were full figured. Tiny knit stocking caps add charm and also keep the egg warm until ready to eat. $45-55.

This photograph shows another group of pedestal-based eggcups. It is not certain whether all were originally sold with knit caps. $45-55.

How do you prepare a perfect 3-minute egg? With an ANRI egg timer, of course. This 5" tall carving was first shown in ANRI trade catalogs during the late 1920s and advertised "for eggs and telephone calls." $75-95.

The lady timer on the left, washtub at her feet, looks as though she's been working hard all day. The "dirt" on her face and clothing is original, adding to her charm. The woman in cleaner clothing on the right must be just beginning her workday. $75-110.

These figures stand 5" tall and would look more appropriate beside a telephone than a stove. They were produced in the late 1920s and have the movable bead/neck feature seen in so many ANRI creations. Less common were timers held by dogs. $75-95.

ANRI made wood and metal bells long before those they produced as Limited Edition collectibles. This dapper man in pink vest and top hat should look familiar to bottle stopper and bar tool collectors. $35-55.

Dinner bells feature both men and women with the same carvings applied to bottle stoppers and bar tools. $35-55.

Toothpick holders and dispensers appear in homes and restaurants all over the world. ANRI made them continuously until the late 1960s, although styles changed. Every ANRI collection should have at least one of these "big mouth" guys that are easy to find. $20-35.

At first they may look alike but all ANRI carvings are one of a kind. Clothing styles and facial features vary and there are men, women, and gnomes. 2" to 3" tall. $20-35.

"Big mouth" toothpick choral groups and choirs make amusing displays.

Some have teeth, others don't. The piece second from the right is hollow and toothpicks are stored and served from his hat. It is also important to note that ANRI toothpick holders and match holders are practically interchangeable. If a small piece of sandpaper is still attached to the bottom, it is meant for matches. $25-45.

A group showing both styles. $25-45.

The first two toothpicks on the left are not ANRI. They may be Swiss carvings.

These little guys are a bit more appealing to ANRI toothpick collectors and it's easy to see why. Clothing styles and faces vary. Toothpicks are stored and served from their hats. $35-65.

By combining figures of people and animals with small barrels, another type of toothpick or match holder was created. $45-60.

This model varies in size depending on the figure but the barrel standard is about 2".

As you can see, the same type of item when added to a base and tin insert becomes an ashtray. $45-75.

ANRI didn't forget man's best friend and many familiar breeds and poses might be found. This St. Bernard stands with his paws against a barrel. $55-75.

Some dog toothpick holders have cleverly carved "baskets" in place of the more common barrels. The two dogs with musical instruments have striking paper on the bottoms indicating that they are match holders. $55-75.

Collectors of ANRI gnomes may find many different models including some with baskets on their backs. The one in the center is more elaborate and would look impressive beside a hearth holding matches. Small gnomes, $35-50, Center model, $65-85.

This gnome sitting on a log is an older carving, produced in the first half of the 1900s. In addition to match and toothpick holders, ANRI used figures like these on several items from pincushions to napkin rings. $45-60.

This model has two gnomes and a larger basket for toothpicks or matches. When this type of carving was fashioned into a pincushion, the basket was stuffed and fabric was applied. The mushrooms served as thimble holders. $45-60.

This style is larger with more attention given to detail. They range from 3" to 4" tall, and while some have a comic quality others are quite realistic. $55-80.

Similar to the previous ones but with less detail. $20-$35.

In this group, the man at left front has a glass insert. Many toothpick holders made from 1912 to the mid-1920s contain a glass insert of some type. $55-80.

This very unusual piece would be suitable as either a match or toothpick holder. It is one of only a few found that incorporate a wooden storage box instead of the typical barrel. The box behind the figure is 1.75" by 1.5" and 2 3/8" tall. The figure is 3.75" tall. $125.

This is a very unusual ANRI piece. The figure is a wooden holder or stand, which originally held a perpetual calendar. The slanted wooden writing surface is for a pad or paper. The head is a removable pencil. 7.75" long, 2 3/8" wide, and 6" tall. $200.

Other ANRI, Other Rooms

There is hardly a single area of a home that couldn't use an object from the workshops of ANRI. Items were created for keeping doors open or closed. Thermometers and barometers gave information about the weather. Boxes were both useful and decorative, and there were brushes for clothing, table, and the hearth.

For the seamstress, there were sewing accessories and ANRI lamps and lighting fixtures were created to illuminate every room. This chapter looks at more of the useful household items ANRI created, each with their unique style and charm.

In old trade catalogs from the mid-1920s, ANRI called this handy item a "door wedge." Today, we are more familiar with the term "doorstop." The tapered, unfinished end of the wedge is pushed beneath the door to keep it stationary. ANRI door wedges have flat bottoms, measure from 4" to 5" long, and were carved with both human and canine figures. $125-130.

This door wedge is different and quite a bit older than the previous two. The black cat is three-dimensional with the wedge tapering down from its back. An ANRI trade catalog from 1921 shows this cat plus a rabbit, an owl, human figures, and several dog breeds. $150.

Doorknockers were another ANRI creation but few have been found to date. This one shows a simple male figure with one carved arm. When the arm is raised and lowered a metal button under the hand meets another one mounted on the back. $125-135.

This doorknocker, seen in both front and side views, has a violinist carved in full figure. ANRI catalog illustrations from 1921 show many figures, some cartoonish in nature, but others more realistic. In addition to human figures catalog pages show a stork, a rabbit, an owl, a penguin, and gnomes. Popular cartoon characters of the era, specifically Krazy Kat, and Bonzo the dog, are also pictured. 4" to 5" tall. $150-175.

In this doorknocker, the man is carved into the top piece of wood with the tongue carved into the piece, which forms the back. When his body is lifted to knock, the tongue seems to go in and out. Maybe it's not the friendliest welcome but it's definitely entertaining. Several models were made with both men and women and even clowns. $150-175.

Thermometers are useful in any room of the house and these two are shown in a 1912 ANRI trade catalog. On the left is a gnome-like creature that resembles a Palmer Cox Brownie, and on the right, a man in distress clutches a tree trunk. Eight different models were pictured in 1921 including mountain climbers, figures with umbrellas, and gnomes. 3" to 5.5" long. $175-200.

Another thermometer, produced in the mid-to-late 1920s, has a male figure similar to the figures seen atop key and pipe racks. $125-150.

By the 1950s new and more colorful designs were being produced. One of the most charming is this "weather tation," which still has its green d gold foil ANRI pine tree label dating from 1954 through 1967. nstructions printed on the back of the item read: "ANRI – Veather Indicator. If you set it to function on a fine day, give the fine weather indicating figure outside. Is it a rainy day give it side by turning the knob on top. Having done so, hang or out it est on a fresh air spot, and never move it. Then it pre-indicates automatically fine or rainy veather, while the corresponding figure comes outside (made in Italy)." [sic] The knob on top of e hat rotates and the eye moves. 10" wide by 12" tall. $200.

ANRI produced several types of brushes for different uses. Some were designed for quick clean up around the fireplace, table, or other small area. 6" to 8.5" long. Dustpans with figural handles were also produced along with the brushes and advertised during the late 1920s. $85-125.

On this clothes brush an adorable Skye terrier sits up as though begging for attention. Illustrations from catalogs printed in 1925 show wirehaired fox terriers, Scottish terriers, spaniels, Pekinese, and other dog breeds. 8" tall. $115.

This monk is also a figural brush, 9" tall. $120.

The figural brush shown here with the brush removed is 8.5" tall. The man in Gröden attire playing a concertina is 6" tall, and the man with applied metal glasses putting on a topcoat is 8" tall. $95-115.

Shown with a page from a 1925 ANRI trade catalog is a carved hairbrush similar in shape and size to metal-backed brushes that are still being produced today. 5" long and 2.5" wide. $75-85.

These interesting items present a bit of a mystery. The characters have movable heads with the neck/bead feature and sit atop boxes that measure 1/8" long by 2.5" wide and 2" tall. The boxes have open ends, similar to bru caddies made during the 1920s. Behind each figur there is another element with slanted sides, 1.5" wide and 1.75" deep, designed to hold another item. What that item was is the mystery. Hopefully someday their purpose may be discovered. $75-8

To date, very few shoehorns have surfaced like this one carved with a dog's head handle produced from 1912 until the beginning of the 1920s. $200+.

Sewing accessories were another group of items produced by the carvers of ANRI. The early catalogs show a huge variety of pincushions, thimble holders, and needle cases but by the end of the 1940s, few were being made. This item is found among illustrations in a catalog from 1921. The base has a hole for storing a thimble and his load of wood was originally stuffed and covered with fabric to form a pincushion. $75-90.

During the 1920s through the 1940s, most sewing items featured gnomes. These two figures are pincushions. The one on the right no longer has its cushion and the gnome on the left is carrying a replacement cushion, not the original. $35-55.

On the other hand, these two have what we believe are the original cushion inserts. Each has a hole for storing a thimble. $45-70.

The object on the left is an ashtray but when seen with the pincushion on the left, the versatility of ANRI figures is obvious. The same gnome on the left may be found as a single item with a pincushion insert. $40-60.

These comical figures are needle cases. They have removable heads and originally the bodies contained a thin wooden insert, a single piece of wood carved into three connected spools for thread. The hollow center of the insert provided a safe place for storing needles or pins. $65-90.

Two little storks come apart mid-body and originally held tiny carved "babies." Other similar toys were produced with very small figural carvings inside, like a cat containing three tiny mice. All these items, which have ANRI labels, were illustrated in trade catalogs printed before1921 and are less than 5" tall. $65-90.

Useful and decorative boxes of all kinds came from the ANRI workshops. These three "twine boxes" open in the center to hold a ball of string. The string is then pulled through a tiny hole in each box top. These were produced in the mid-to-late 1920s and measure 4" by 5". Many models were made including gnomes. $155-175.

This little jewelry box is both useful and decorative, made entirely of wood, and has a carved figural knob on top. The box itself is 3" diameter and 1.5" tall. The tiny carved figure is an additional 1.5" tall. This piece was produced before 1930. $125-150.

A totally different kind of jewelry or item box is this lady with her umbrella. Made to hold small objects, it stands 7" tall to the top of her umbrella and the box is 2.5" diameter. $65-75.

These ANRI boxes could be used to store anything from pins and stamps to pills. The largest is 3.5" square, 1.5" deep. The Indian box is 1.5" diameter, 1" deep and the small man box is 2" diameter, 1.5" deep. $95-125.

This box is carved in bas-relief with a religious figure. 6.25" long. $100.

This lamp has a young Alpine boy with a guitar and measures 7" tall to the socket. The base is 4.75" wide and just under 2" deep. $275-300.

Few people are aware that ANRI also produced lamps and light fixtures but early ANRI catalogs show several pages with different models. This table lamp features a tuba player and is 11" tall to the socket. The base is 4" wide, 5.25" deep, and the figure is 6.25" tall. The same musician was sold as a figurine without the lamp. $275-300.

A pair of Gröden citizens in festive native attire decorates this lamp. 8" tall to the socket. The base is slightly less than 4" square, and the figures are 4.5" tall. $275-300

Gnomes were also used on ANRI lamps like this one playing a concertina. 8" tall to the socket. The base is 4.25" wide, 3.5" deep. The figure is 5" tall. $250-275.

In the early 1920s six light fixtures were commissioned for a new Philadelphia pub. The fixtures hung over booths in the bar until the building was being torn down in the 1960s. Four of the fixtures were purchased by one gentleman and put into storage until the late 1980s. He then sold two of those four to a man in Florida where they were again stored, until they were offered at auction in 1995.

Each fixture is shown front and back. One has two men toasting each other with mugs of beer and the other features men playing horns. Each of the light fixtures is 17" tall and 22" wide.

Luckily, we know what was carved on two more of the original six. One depicted a bear standing on its hind legs facing a hunter with a gun, and the other had a drunken man facing his angry wife with a rolling pin raised above her head. Sadly, the fate of the other two fixtures is unknown.

Hang It Up

The ANRI carvers produced a variety of wall racks and wall hooks for hanging keys, pipes, matches, ties, and clothing. All featured figural carvings of people or animals.

Racks with one, two, or three figures for hanging pipes and keys were produced continuously from the mid-1920s through the 1960s. Wall hooks for clothing and tie racks had a shorter production span of only a few decades. Spoon racks didn't appear until the mid-1950s. With key racks, the numbers of small metal hooks determined the length of the rack.

As the 1950s ended the demand had dwindled until only a few styles of key racks were being made.

Single figure racks measure approximately 6" long and 4" tall. Both male and female figures were used and in all models the neck/bead system was used to make the heads movable. $45-55.

This model has a male character holding a musical instrument. The hooks are atypical and likely replacements for the originals. $35-45.

Some single character key racks show the figure carved with arms crossed and resting along the top of the "fence" or top edge of the rack itself. $45-55.

Key racks with two figures may vary in dress and carving style as seen in these two examples. Each has hooks for 4 keys and is about 8" in length. $45-65.

This older, two figure key rack is unusual because the hooks are inserted into a bar extending across the rack itself. It was produced in the late 1920s to late 1940s. $65-75.

The carving and style of this key rack is much older than those shown previously and was likely produced before the 1920s. $85-95.

Models with three characters usually have one female and two male figures. Clothing styles vary and the addition of musical instruments may also be found. These three figure racks are about 12" long. $75-85.

This key rack with three figures shows a man playing a concertina and a woman with a guitar. The remaining male is holding a bouquet of flowers. $55-85.

In a completely different style, this key rack has four characters carved in full figure standing along the top edge. $55-85.

This photograph shows another group of key racks and the variety of figures that may be found. $45-75.

This rack features the same Alpine children seen on napkin rings and other items. Six of them are peering over a fence with four hooks. $55-75.

A whimsical four hook rack with two alpine children sitting on a wall beneath an umbrella. $55-75.

ANRI introduced this model, shaped like a big key, during the 1950s. A male figure in a top hat that resembles comic actor W. C. Fields is standard. He's always seen holding a lantern in his right hand. There are four hooks for hanging keys. Model variants include color and finish of the wooden key, as well as different shaped and colored lanterns. 14" long. $75-95.

Racks for holding small spoons were another household item ANRI produced beginning in the mid-1950s. Small slots were carved into a wooden bar and two figures were applied. Each holds five spoons and is about 6" long. $40-65.

Another type of wall rack ANRI produced was for hanging tobacco pipes. This three-figure model is 12" long, but smaller racks were also made that measured from 6" to 8" long. $60-90.

The ANRI carvers made tie bars or racks from the 1920s through the mid-to-late 1940s, but few if any were being produced when ANRI trade catalogs were printed in the 1950s. Between one and three figures were added to racks ranging in length from 6" to 12". $75-95.

Most figures on ANRI racks have the neck/bead feature making it possible to turn the heads in all directions. Due to age, the string holding the pieces together is often broken and the heads may be found glued down and immovable. It is important to note that this does not devalue the items to a large degree but to be considered "mint," the heads must still be movable. $85-100.

Tie bars with three figures, produced between 1925 and the late 1940s, show the variety of faces carved. 12" long. $85-120.

Occasionally, ANRI racks may be found with wooden hooks or pegs instead of metal ones but they are less common. These were used to hang everything from kitchen towels to clothing. $75-95.

Two uncommon tie racks shown here feature dogs. The first has a Scottish terrier and another mysterious breed of dog applied to a wooden bar. It measures 11.5" long and 2.5" deep. The second also has two carved dogs but with metal rings. Dogs were also featured on key racks and pipe racks. $100-125.

This interesting wall box is divided into three shallow compartments that may have been used for spices, matches, or other items. It was produced in the early 1920s and retains an ANRI label. 8" long by 3" deep. $100-125.

Most wall hooks had realistic figural carvings of men and women in natural poses. Wall hooks are 5" to 6" long. A slightly larger model was produced that included a shelf with the figures underneath (not shown). $175-200.

Some wall hook figures hold musical instruments like the concertina seen here, but guitars were also carved. Women may be found holding infants or with knitting needles and yarn. Other examples were more comical like the figure in the big hat on the right. $175-200.

ANRI wall hooks are wonderful items and extremely difficult to find. They were pictured in a trade catalog from 1921, but mysteriously disappeared from subsequent printings. $175-200.

This wall hook has lost an arm so we can only imagine what it once held. Even so, the quality and detail of the carving is still impressive and this one was probably produced before 1920.

Here are two examples of hanging wall boxes commonly used to hold matches. The piece on the left is obviously an ANRI carving. The box on the right is probably a German carving. The ANRI matchbox is 9" tall. $75-90.

Nutcrackers

ANRI began showing nutcrackers in their trade catalogs as early as 1921. In fact, the early catalogs have as many as five pages of illustrations with thirty different nutcrackers pictured. Of those, twenty-one were animals and birds and only nine had carvings of people.

Two different styles or types of nutcrackers were available at that time. The "pliers" type has a backward-curving front handle and a straight back handle. The fully carved figure on a round wooden pedestal base that allows it to stand upright has a straight handle in back. Both types were designed so that a nut was placed into a hole in back and cracked by pulling down on the back handle.

The freestanding nutcrackers were whimsical, toy-like creatures with painted clothing and included a penguin, a rabbit, a mouse, an owl, and several generic birds.

The pliers type animals had bodies partially carved into the front handle. A hound, rabbit, monkey, rooster, and bulldog are shown carved to neck level in realistic fashion. Eight others have more detailed bodies carved further down along the front handle. Some are even dressed in clothing with hats and scarves including a parrot, mouse, elephant, pig, cat, dog, and two generic birds.

The remaining illustrations in the 1921 catalog show human figures including a gnome, and a monk with a snuffbox.

ANRI nutcrackers measure from 7" to 8" long and feature mouths that open and close when the back handle is raised and lowered. When users mistakenly attempted to crack nuts with the mouths, the bottom jaws were often broken or chipped, like the lady in brown on the left. $300-350.

So many interesting faces were carved that a nutcracker display seems like a portrait gallery of Gröden Valley villagers. $300-350.

This wonderful nutcracker not only opens and closes its mouth but the eyes also change from blue to brown when the handle is lifted. $400.

In this threesome, the man on the left also has the changing eye color feature seen in the previous nutcracker. $300-400.

Another handsome threesome. $300-400.

By the mid-1920s another style of nutcracker had been added to the ANRI trade catalog pages. They were a similar pliers type but the front handle resembled a fishtail that allowed them to stand upright without assistance. $300-350.

The monk with the fishtail handle on the right is holding a snuffbox in his left hand. $300-350.

Some ANRI nutcrackers were left unpainted like the one second from the left. $300-350.

American Indian. $375.

Opposite page: Again, we see the addition of inserted glass or plastic eyes in these four nutcrackers. The two on the left are a mountain goat and an unpainted chamois. On the right are two very similar "hound" type dogs. Notice that only the two painted models have the fishtail front handle. $350-400.

Tyrolean characters. $375.

Both of these nutcrackers were produced in the early 1920s. Glass eyes were added to some models like the owl although one has been damaged. Inset glass or plastic eyes do not increase the value to a large degree but they do, in most cases, identify older carvings. $350-400.

In ANRI trade catalogs printed in the middle to late 1920s and continuing through the early 1950s, the number of different nutcracker characters had dwindled. The dog breeds pictured were Skye terriers, Scottish terriers, wirehaired Fox terriers, and few others. It is also important to note that only "fish tail" models were illustrated. $350-400.

By the mid-to-late 1950s only one style of nutcracker was illustrated in the ANRI trade catalogs. This model featured a fully carved, free standing Gröden Valley citizen with a straight back handle. This chef or cook is shown in a catalog printed in 1956. $300-350.

These two Gröden Valley gentlemen are shown in a 1956 ANRI catalog. The value of these models is consistent with earlier models because fewer were produced. Sadly, by the 1960s, ANRI no longer offered nutcrackers in their trade catalogs. $300-350.

This rare ANRI nutcracker is carved to represent a cartoon dog from the 1920s called Bonzo. Collectors must compete with those who collect Bonzo exclusively. ANRI also produced Bonzo bottle stoppers, napkin rings, and pincushions. $550-750.

Another very early ANRI nutcracker is this black cat with an attached nut dish. The bowl is 9.25" diameter, and less than 2" tall. The cat figure is 4 3/8" tall. 6" overall height. $350-400.

The last of our ANRI nutcrackers is not pictured in any available trade catalogs. It is 7" tall, 6" wide, and 5" deep. A handle in the back moves the jaw. Truly a work of art. $500.

Part Three

ANRI for the Bar

Today, by acclamation, bar items are the most popular vintage items ANRI produced. Something about them appeals to both drinkers and non-drinkers.

The first item ever produced by ANRI was a bottle stopper and these stoppers are still sought after today. It was Eduard Mahlknecht, along with Anton Riffeser, who developed the creation of wooden carvings atop bottle corks from which the whole industry began.

In addition to stoppers, ANRI bar pieces included pourers, bottle cappers, corkscrews, bottle openers or cap lifters, and bar sets containing several tools, some with cork coasters. There were also elaborate bar scenes or dioramas with multiple figures combining a number of tools and accessories.

The last bottle stopper or bar accessory was produced in 1976.

Collectors often ask how many different types of bottle stoppers ANRI produced. The answer is, no one knows. Records show that hundreds were made of each model and there were hundreds of models. Numbers don't matter, for as we all know, a true collector never stops or declares his collection complete.

There are two types of bottle stoppers: "stills" or non-mechanicals and "mechanicals." The first non-mechanical stoppers portrayed men and women in native attire and were of simple design. In the 1930s the motifs were expanded to include realistic dogs, dressed animals, fruits and vegetables, and others ranging in size from 3"-5" including the original 1.5" tapered corks.

Since many bottle stoppers today are found with missing, broken, or replaced corks, the measurements given in this section exclude the cork unless otherwise noted. A mint condition bottle stopper should retain its original cork but little value is lost because of cork damage.

Non-mechanical bottle stoppers may be very realistic or comical "caricatures" of people or animals. $35-45.

Stoppers may be intricately carved or very simple, almost crude. Originally, ANRI sold the more detailed, finely carved stoppers at a higher price due to the work involved, but today's collectors don't seem concerned with price. They want them all. $30-40.

Happy faces with applied wire eyeglasses. $35-55.

Both realistic and caricature stoppers are illustrated here. $35-55.

There are a variety of interesting carvings to be found in addition to the locals from Tyrol, like American Indians, Jamaican police officers, and figures in military uniforms from around the world. $60-75.

This is an early intricate carving with finely detailed painting. Later models have rounded, dowel shaped bodies and their faces are less skillfully carved. $55-65.

Notice the detailed clothing and deeply carved mouths on the stoppers to the left and right compared to the one in the center. $55-85.

While the lady may look like a Dutch girl, her hat is actually part of the traditional clothing of the Gröden Valley. The man has the beautifully detailed face that collectors prize. He's so cheerful and appealing he might remind you of a favorite uncle. $55-75.

It's hard to know whether this fellow is singing or yelling. He might even have been carved mid-yawn. Stoppers with deeply carved, open or partially open mouths, are especially charming. $55-65.

This type of stopper, measured without the cork, ranges in size from 2.5" to 4" tall. $30-65.

ANRI offered dozens of breeds of dogs, cats, bears, squirrels, elephants, rabbits, mice, and many more. $45-60.

ANRI animal stoppers may be carved in full figure or with only the animals' heads. Dogs, $45-65; squirrels, $35-55; bears, $55-75; other animals, $45-65.

These small dog stoppers, less than 2" tall, are uncommon, but not as appealing as the more detailed, larger examples. It was noted in ANRI catalogs that these and other stoppers of this size were for "smaller flasks." $15-25.

The oldest known animal stoppers were a series with carved clothing. They included a frog, rabbit, mouse, turtle, stork, pig, and rooster. Some wore hats and applied metal glasses. Although this type of stopper has a pivoting head due to an additional wooden bead between the head and shoulders, it is still classified as non-mechanical. $300-350.

These very old gentlemen with applied fabric collars and ties were produced from the late 1920s until the mid-1930s. They feature the same pivoting neck as the dressed animal series and a stem-like, carved pedestal base. Women may also be found but fewer were produced. $100-150.

Other models may be found with an unusual stem base. This older male figure in a traditional brimless cap was produced in the early 1920s. $100-125.

Full figure, non-mechanical stoppers illustrate the true talent of the ANRI carvers and the excellent quality of their work. Each tiny figure is a work of art. Both painted and unpainted figures were produced. $95-115.

Men and women in Tyrolean dress, gnomes, musicians, and realistic caricature carvings are among the many ANRI stoppers. $75-95.

It was noted in old ANRI trade catalogs that "hundreds" of stopper designs were available in all styles. The variety and detail, not to mention the sheer numbers produced, boggles the imagination. $75-95.

The Big Three

If you've been collecting for any length of time, you know that there are three mechanical bottle stoppers that no collection is complete without. They are the "hat tipper," the "kissing couple," and the "drinking man." Although relatively easy to find, there are a variety of different styles in all three models, so gather several of each. As in all ANRI creations, each is one of a kind. No two are ever exactly alike.

We move into the mechanical stopper category with the hat tipper. A unique aspect found in hat tippers is that movement is provided by a pull-string, rather than a lever or twist peg. Few other models use the pull string mechanism. A mint hat tipper should rest with the hat on top of the head, and bow and tip the hat when the string is pulled. Once the string is released, the hat and head should return to the original positions. $45-65.

Hat tippers may be found in a variety of clothing styles and colors. Some hold objects in the left hand. $45-65.

A left handed hat tipper is yet to be found, but a very unusual "double hat tipper" appears on the right. When the string is pulled, both men tip their hats. Double hat tipper, $150.

Values vary depending on age and quality of carving. $45-65.

Above: Nothing is as romantic as a kiss and ANRI paid tribute to love and romance with their "Kissing Couple" bottle stopper. The most common example has a lady on the right and a gentleman on the left carved from about the waist up and side-by-side. A couple with the man on the right side of the woman is shown (left) but closer examination of the clothing proves the heads have somehow been reversed. Pressing down on the wooden lever in back causes the figures to turn their heads toward each other and kiss. Releasing the lever should bring them back to their original positions, facing forward. Kissing couples are still being produced in the Tyrol, but not by ANRI. They are of poor quality, crudely carved, and painted in very bright colors. $45-65.

Center: In older models, as with all ANRI stoppers, the clothing was carved in great detail, and tiny patterns were often painted on blouses and scarves. Older faces are sweet and appealing, while newer, less skillfully carved faces seem stern or comical with overly exaggerated lips. It is not uncommon to find kissing couples that function perfectly but don't actually find their target when they kiss. We don't penalize them for this. $45-65.

A more unusual kissing couple is carved in full figure seated side by side. This model called "Happy End" in an old ANRI catalog incorporates the hat-tipping feature. When the lever is manipulated, the man doffs his cap and kisses his lady fair. $55-75.

Kissing couple-hat tippers have wooden levers (left and right). Some kissing couples were carved holding hands (center). $45-65.

The rarest kissing couple is the "face-to-face" model that is carved with the man's arms on the lady's shoulders. $150-175.

The drinking man is another of ANRI's common models and the last of the "big three." As seen here, the quality of carving varies. A mint drinking man should hold a mug, cup, bottle, or stein in his right hand and when the wooden lever in back is depressed, he should raise the vessel to his mouth as the mouth opens. Releasing the lever should bring the right arm back to his side and the mouth should close. Crude imitations of this model are still being produced in the Tyrol region but not by ANRI. $55-65.

Using the same type of movement as the hat tipper, ANRI made a wonderful variety of stoppers that do all kinds of interesting things when the levers are depressed. The two on the left answer telephones. The one on the right puts a camera up to his eye. Notice that one of the telephone stoppers is an unusual left-handed version. $45-75.

Here are four mechanical musician stoppers. The drummers alternate lifting their right and left hands as if to beat the drums. The concertina player tilts his head from side to side while the left hand moves out and away from the body to simulate play. The violinist, who is less common, tilts his from side to side while the right hand draws his bow across the fiddle. $55-75.

The train conductor lifts a signal light with his right hand, the reader puts on metal glasses as he lowers his head, and the chef lifts a wooden spoon. $45-65.

Two uncommon women stoppers wield a rolling pin and an old-fashioned rug beater. $65-75.

Lacking a better description, collectors call this particular model the "Yakker" or talking stopper that was made in two different styles. In one the mouth simply opens when the lever is depressed, while in the other, the head lifts up from the shoulders as the mouth opens (far left). These yakkers were carved from the waist up and are shown here with mouths opened and closed. $45-65.

Full figured yakkers are especially nice and have many different clothing styles. Both men and women may be found but the ladies are less common. $55-75

This yakker was made in the late 1920s to mid-1940s and has "Quebec," painted on the base indicating that it had been exported for sale in Canada. Painted city names and souvenir decals are frequently found on ANRI carvings. The eyes on this stopper show the skill and attention to detail found in older ANRI stoppers. $80.

Here is another nice group of yakkers shown with mouths closed and opened. $55-65.

At first, these photographs seem to show eight different stoppers. Actually, they are the same four stoppers seen from opposite sides. This "two faced hat flipper" is carved with a face on each side, but one is always hidden behind a hat. The hats are attached so that they flip back and forth revealing the different faces. Combinations of facial features depicting happy/sad, old/young, black/white, male/female may be found with many different types of hats. Collectors should beware of reproductions recently seen on Internet auction sites. $85-120.

One of the strangest ANRI stoppers is the hidden head, or "head in head" model. Depressing the lever in back causes the hat on the stopper to lift up as a smaller head/face rises from inside. The small face may be painted on a round wooden bead or it may be fully carved and painted. Carved faces are more desirable, although both are fun. Another model, not shown, has a small bird inside the main figure's head which one collector dubbed a "bird brained" stopper. $55-75.

Below: An uncommon Santa Claus "head in head" figure, painted bright red and white, can be seen in the center of this photograph. ANRI may not have meant for this model to be associated with St. Nick, but it is commonly recognized as such. Santa, $75-100. The stopper on the right is called a "dead eye" because of the scarf tied around the head and over one eye. This one is also a "head in head" stopper, but others may be found without this feature. $65-85.

Here is another strangely wonderful model that is hard to describe so collectors call it, the stopper that "sticks out its tongue." Doesn't exactly roll *off* the tongue, does it? At any rate, it is a collector favorite. These photographs show the stoppers at rest and as they look when a thin wooden peg at the back of the head is pushed inward making the tongues stick out and the eyes roll up. $45-60.

Here's another one that is difficult to label but fun to own. The four gentlemen look relatively plain but when the levers are depressed the mouths open and the eyes close. This type is called a "blinker." $45-65.

Here are three examples of stoppers with "roaming eyes." At rest, they look straight ahead. Male stoppers have a cigar or cigarette in their mouths while lady stoppers were non-smokers. Built into the head is a thin peg that is manipulated by sliding it horizontally from side to side. This causes the man's hat to spin, the eyes to move left to right, and the cigar to shift slightly. The woman's lever is built into her shoulders and when moved, her eyes go from blue to brown, her mouth acquires a toothy grin, and she changes from having a shirt collar to a pale green scarf. Another difference is that the lever can be left in either position. Beware of fake blinkers and roaming eye stoppers recently seen on Internet auction sites. Males, $55-65. Ladies, $65-75.

Although these monkeys are technically hat tippers, they are more difficult to find. Faces and attire vary but basically it is a monkey sitting on its haunches with a cup in the left hand. Instead of a pulling a string, one pushes down on a carved tail and, like organ grinder monkeys of old, off comes the hat as it begs for a coin. $95-125.

Here is a different kind of monkey holding a cup in both hands but this one doesn't have a wardrobe or cap. Depressing the lever in back brings the cup to its mouth. $75-100.

During frontier times, Black cavalrymen who became cowboys after completing military service were called Buffalo Soldiers. ANRI produced two models, both with real leather hats or hat brims. The model on the right carries a rifle under the left arm and tips its hat. Interestingly, the rifle is carved with the barrel pointing backward. Not good gun safety, but it's doubtful the carvers thought about that. On the left, the hat moves from the back of the head to a more forward position over the brow. Both have wooden levers that produce movement. $75-90.

Here is another pair of unusual ANRI stoppers that have the "string-pull" mechanism. On the left, a man and woman hold a cup or a mug. When the string is pulled, they swing away from each other and when the string is released, they return to center, clicking their glasses together in a toast. Salute! $60-80. The couple on the left is not as happy. Each holds a broom and when the string is pulled the figures swing away from each other. When the string is released the figures return to center, hitting each other with the brooms. Collectors call this stopper "Punch and Judy." Whack! $65-85.

No collection is complete without elephants and donkeys (next photograph). The elephants are designed so that lifting the tail causes the head to rise and the ears to flop back and forth. They also have an atypical square base. $55-75.

The center donkey is designed like the elephants seen in the previous photograph. Lifting the tail causes the head to rise and the ears to flop. This donkey and the elephants were introduced in 1948 and may have represented the two American political parties. The donkeys on the left and right were introduced in 1949, have round bases, and twist peg motion. When manipulated the head lowers, the ears flop forward, and the hind legs "kick" out. Beneath the hooves a small sign may be found. Signs are examined further in the following photos. $55-75.

Stopper collectors love surprises and this category offers more than its share. These animals have small paper signs attached to their feet. The signs are face down but when a peg is twisted or a tail is pressed, the animal sits or stands up on two legs and the signs can be read. When the rooster's tail is lifted, one leg kicks up to reveal a sign. Each sign has a one or two word drinking toast. "Your Health," "Cheers," "Bottoms Up," "Cin-Cin," and "Prosit" have been found. Stoppers without the original signs have less value. Rooster, $65-80; dogs, $65-80; donkeys, $55-75. Beware of fake ANRI roosters on the market today. They are similar in appearance, made of a light unfinished wood, and have only red painted accents instead of several colors.

As noted earlier, the "twist peg" is a small wooden dowel inserted into the base of a stopper. When the peg is twisted, figures move in a variety of ways. This example is a fully carved figure of a man holding a cup in one hand and a wine bottle in the other, a more complex example of the common, drinking man bottle stopper. When manipulated, he bends at the waist and his left arm rises in a pouring motion. Twisting the peg in the opposite direction causes him to bend backwards slightly bringing the right arm up and the cup to his mouth. At 5.25" tall including the base, this is one of the tallest ANRI stoppers. Twist peg drinker, $75-85.

Another great drinking stopper with twist peg action is this ANRI drinking bear, which is similar to the drinking monkey stopper seen earlier. The bear is holding a bottle that is the only painted element on this model. 4" tall including base. $80-95.

ANRI collectors call this stopper the "Gentleman Caller" or "Courting Man." Not quite 5" tall, he holds a bouquet of posies in his left hand and the brim of his top hat in the other. When the peg is twisted, he bows from the waist and tips his hat. The second photograph shows an older model with what's left of an original fabric top hat. It is easy to see why the felt hats were soon replaced with wooden hats. $85-95.

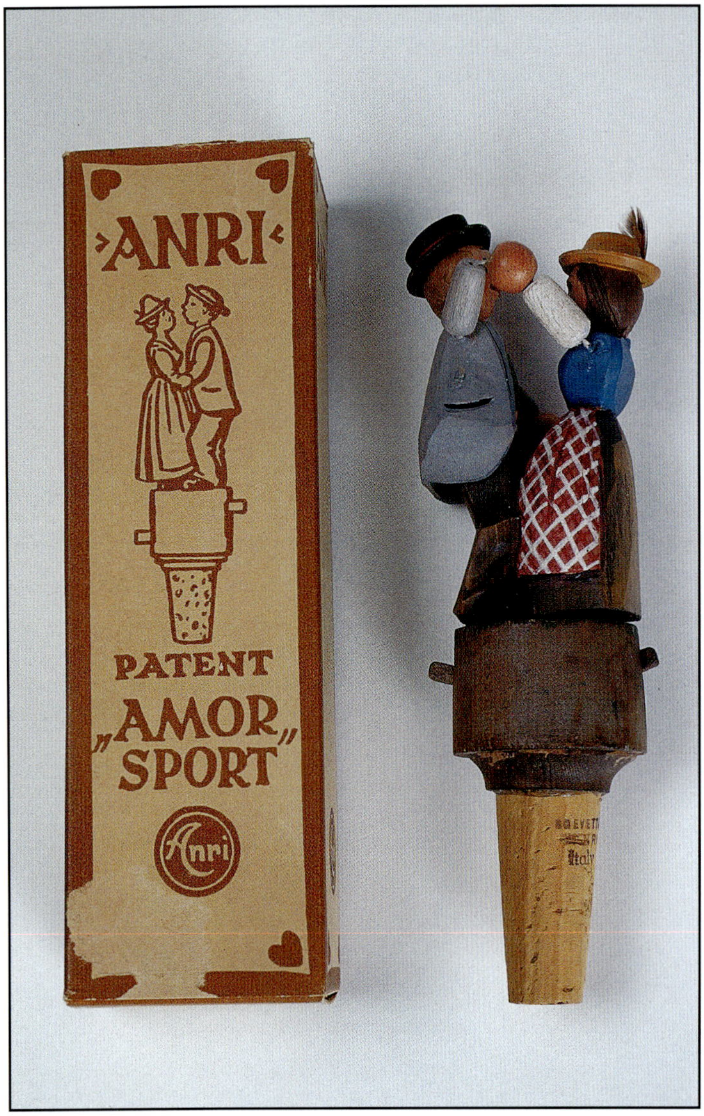

ANRI didn't name many bottle stoppers but this one is called "Amor Sport." The only double peg stopper, it features a man and woman standing face-to-face holding hands.

Manipulating the two pegs brings the faces of these couples closer together and, depending on agility and whim, they may kiss. Some of the ladies have a real feather in their hats. $85-100. MIB $175-200.

The word "tipple" is seldom used anymore but it means, "to habitually drink alcoholic beverages." Tipplers are heavy drinkers or, in modern terms, drunks. The "Tipple Tipple" stopper is a fully carved male figure with an umbrella under one arm and bottle of booze in hand. It features what resembles a twist peg but the peg is pushed inward which causes him to bob and sway in a drunken fashion. Umbrellas may be found in different colors and at least one figure has been found wearing a black top hat. Notice that on the original box the illustration indicates that the peg twists but this is an error. 5" tall. $85-100. MIB, $175-200.

One of best-loved, most coveted stoppers ANRI created is the Ballerina. ANRI trade catalogs refer to her as "dancing girl." She stands on her toes atop a round base and has painted laces above her shoes. Lacey pantaloons or panties are painted on beneath her skirt. Two different movements involved in this series are accomplished with a twist peg. In one type, the figure tilts front to back in a "curtsey" movement, while the second type tilts from the waist, side-to-side. Each has thin arms with small applied hands. To make things even more interesting the dresses were painted in several different colors so a complete set would necessarily include one of each available color, in *each* of the two movements. Colors found include, red, royal blue, baby blue, white, yellow, mint green, emerald green, and black. 4.5" tall including base. $95-150.

It was surprising to lear that ANRI named this model, "Knockout." Er Riffeser was asked how got the name and he replied, "It is very difficult to translate wha the figurines are doing. We could say that the m are drunk and that they are out of action, they have given up." He actually explains it very well. "Knockout," migh well be called, "passed out." Eduard Mahlknec was the creator and it w produced between 1954 and 1962. Each figure si atop a road sign, similar modern day "mile markers," which is, presumably, where they "gave up." Twisting the peg makes them fall drunkenly back and fort Kilometer numbers var from one example to the next. $85-110.

Two of the cutest bottle stoppers ANRI produced are the acrobatic monkey and gnome. The monkey is always dressed in red pants, a blue jacket, and a red hat. The gnome with a turned up nose is less colorful but just as charming in a peaked cap. The monkey has an applied metal tail that curls up onto his back.

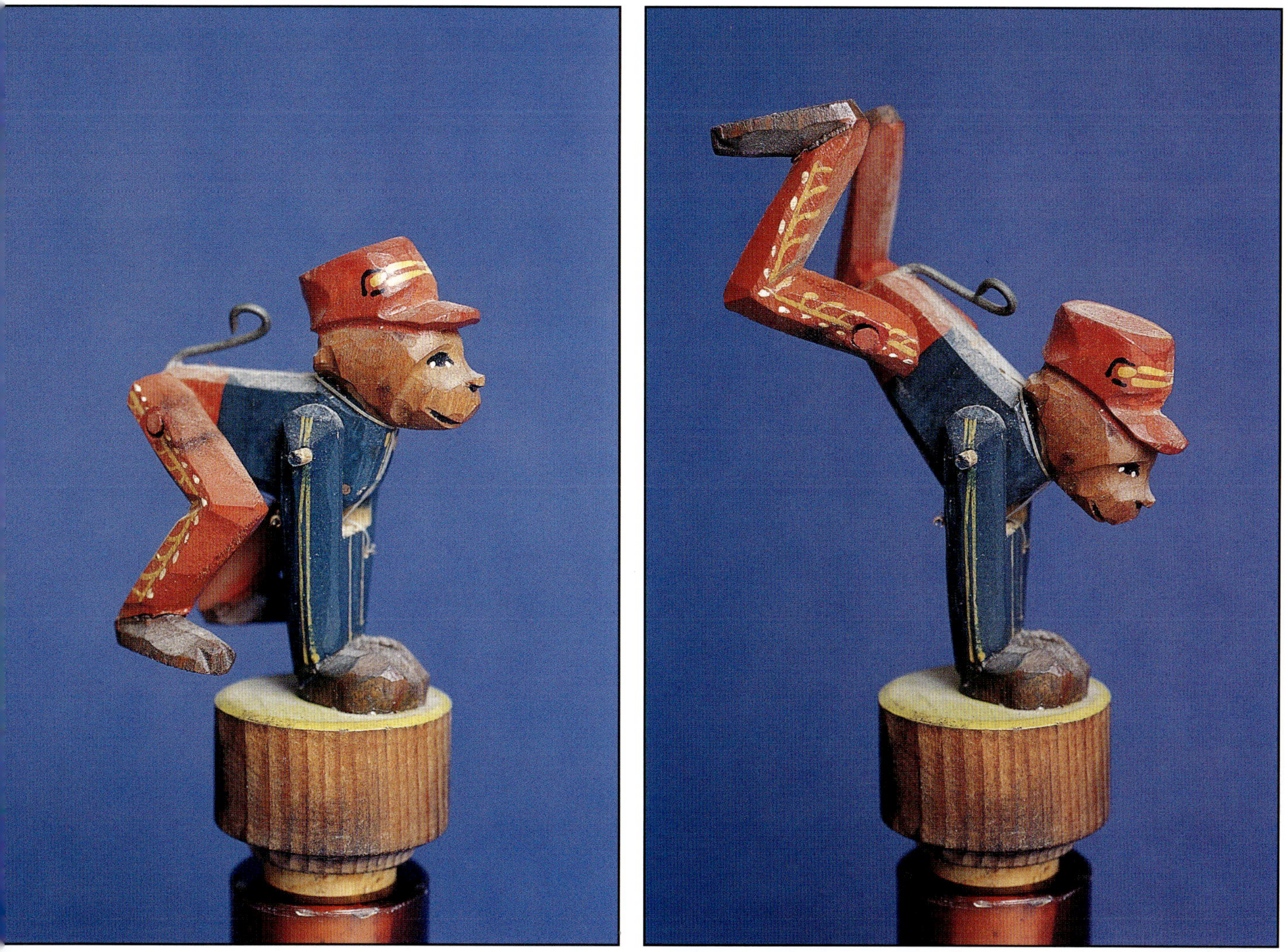

At rest, these figures are balanced on their hands and when the peg is twisted, their lower bodies rise and both legs flip into the air as they do a handstand. $150-175+.

These two models weren't made until the early to mid-1950s, placing them into the final years of ANRI stopper production. They are extremely popular with collectors and, why not? They conjure up memories of 1950s Westerns and the cowboy heroes of our youth. On the left is a cowboy riding an Appaloosa pony and carrying a rifle over his shoulder. He hangs on while his steed rears up on hind legs when the peg is twisted. The cowboy with a pistol in each hand is ready for "High Noon." Twisting the peg causes him to raise and lower alternating arms, and tilt his head from side to side. $125-150+.

In ANRI catalogs, this stopper was called "Take It Easy." The man seems to have come home carrying a bottle in one hand and the door key in the other. The peg is pushed back and forth causing the figure to sway drunkenly. After several practice attempts the key may be guided to the keyhole in the door. $125-150+. With the following bottle stopper we see what happens next.

What was waiting for the man just behind the door? This model called "Buon Giorno," has the answer. There stands a lady (we can presume it's his wife) holding a shoe in her right hand. Part of a man's face and one foot, is visible just past the threshold of the door. When the peg is twisted, her arm rises and his head moves forward becoming fully visible beyond the door. When the peg is twisted the opposite way, her arm with shoe in hand, comes back down just as his head pulls back safely out of reach. What a way to say, "Good Morning!" This one is 4.5" tall and has a 1925 ANRI label on the bottom of the cork. $200+.

Called "A Happy Drunk" in ANRI trade catalogs, this is another stopper that collectors love but it is hard to find. It features a man with one hand atop a beer barrel and the other holding a cup or stein. Pressing the wooden peg makes him bend and sway in a typical drunken manner. 5" tall including base. $95-125.

A line in an old drinking song inspired this stopper. A figure hangs onto a signpost with one hand and keeps a tight grip on a wine bottle in the other. Pushing the wooden peg back and forth makes him jiggle around like the drunkard he is. This model may be found with the message "Show Me the Way Home," printed in several languages. 4.5" tall including base. $85-110.

Monks were a favorite ANRI theme and several types of bottle stopper models were produced with monks featured. The HB painted on the stein held by the full figured monk and other ANRI carvings stands for *Hofbrauhaus*, the German word for Beer Garden. They do not signify a specific brewery or establishment. $35-55.

Here are three different types of monk stoppers showing some of the carving styles that were produced. The monk on the right is a Yakker or "talking" stopper. $45-70.

A push puppet is a toy in which the parts of a figure are strung with elastic cord and held in place by the cord's tension. When the base is depressed, the tension is released and the figure collapses. Releasing the base again puts tension on the cord and the figure springs back in place. This type incorporates push puppet toys made by ANRI in the early years with a functional cork bottle stopper. In addition to the models seen here, others were produced including some with animals. Here are two drunks with bottles and a couple in Alpine clothing. 4" to 5" tall including base. $75-85.

This unusual push puppet features the familiar drunk holding onto a lamppost. When the top of the lamp is pressed downward, tension on the elastic co[r]d is released and the figure collapses. $85-90.

Probably a rare advertising give-away, this Mumm champagne bottle is another push puppet. Mumm began making bubbly in France in 1827 and is still in operation today. When the "stopper" on the top of the bottle is depressed, a door on the back opens and a little monkey peeks out. Seems to say that champagne can make a monkey out of you. $350.

This is an example of another kind of push puppet. Pushing down on its head causes both arms to raise and lower. $75-85.

Pictured in catalogs from the 1920s, these stoppers are made of a series of beads tightly strung with string rather than elastic cord. They remain basically fixed but are movable to some degree. $200-250.

There were several models produced in this series including a man holding a guitar, several with metal canes, and some holding steins. $200-250.

At first, the collector who found this believed it was simply an ugly stopper made by someone who probably flunked out of carving school. But happily, it was later found to be one of many ANRI stoppers of this type produced in the early 1920s. This model has metal buttons on the clothing and protruding wooden peg noses may be found. The heads rotate on a bead/neck above the body. $85-100.

A peg inserted to represent the nose may be seen in other models like these two examples from the late 1920s. $75-95.

For lack of a better name these little people are called, "Alpine children." One collector who doesn't care for them, calls them "pinhole eyed kids" because most of them have a tiny "pinhole" where the pupil of the eye would be. Most collectors like these little characters with their colorful clothing and carefree personalities. $35-55.

Alpine children may be found holding musical instruments, hiking, carrying flowers, or just sitting around on top of beer barrels. In other words, they are just like the other ANRI carvings in variety and imagination. These are the same little folks found decorating ANRI napkin rings. But be aware that not all Alpine children were produced and sold by ANRI. Several carvers produced and sold them all over the Tyrol region during the 1940s and 1950s. Alpine Kids and Kids On Kegs, $35-45.

An Alpine boy serenades his girlfriend who is playing a concertina. $35-40.

Not all figures sitting on top of barrels are Alpine children. The beer barrel, as with all drink related themes, is a staple in ANRI bottle stoppers. Watch for different kinds of figures on or in kegs. Hat tippers on barrels are not as common but don't seem to spark the same interest with collectors. $30-45.

Here is what would be an ordinary hat tipper except for the addition of a lower body complete with legs, dressed in fabric pants. This is a "fantasy" and was created by a past owner for his or her own amusement. $45.

Another unusual ANRI stopper is this one depicting a pair of mountain climbers, one atop the peak and the other dangling from a "rope" below. Pulling the string raises and lowers the bottom climber. $225.

In the late 1920s through early 1950s, ANRI produced a series of stoppers and pourers depicting Bacchus, the Greek Dionysus, god of wine and song. These were advertised as the "finest carvings made from precious woods." Today, they are still some of the most beautiful ANRI pieces. $250-275.

The stoppers in the rack shown here come from two different series of stoppers shown in vintage catalogs from the 1950s. On the left and right are two very detailed carvings that ANRI considered their "finest quality." The center stopper is an oriental man holding a paper fan. He is one of six models in the "International Collection" which were figures carved in native costumes from around the world. $75-100.

There were six figures in the Bacchus series, which may be found as both stoppers and pourers, and in natural or painted wood. Some pourers had nickel-plated collars and the heads remove to expose the spouts inside. Pourers are examined further in the next chapter of this book. $250+.

The Dickens Characters

Today, no series of bottle stoppers or figurines produced by ANRI are more sought after than the Charles Dickens set. There were eleven characters shown in a catalog produced in the late 1930s and early 1940s, but at least thirteen were produced. They are: "David Copperfield," "Mr. Pickwick," "Dolly Varden," "Mr. Pecksniff," "Captain (Capt.) Cuttle," "Mrs. (or Sarah or Sairy) Gamp," the "Artful Dodger," "Joe the Fat Boy," "Sam Weller," "Jacob (Job.) Trotter," "Mr. Dick," and "Mr. Micawber." It is also possible that a "Little Nell" stopper exists, although to date, none has been found, but recently a stopper of "Trotty Veck" was discovered. Each, $275+. Complete Set, $$$$!

Rather than call this type of item a bottle stopper, it is referred to as a bottle "capper." These figures are fashioned with a cork hidden inside the carving. The entire carving fits tightly around the top of the bottle and the cork fits into the neck. $75-100.

Some older ANRI stoppers were sold with matching stands with articulated legs. Once the stopper is placed inside, it becomes a fully carved, seated figure, and some were quite imaginative. The man inserted in the barrel is not original to this model but a replacement. The figure to the left in the right photograph is also a "head in head" stopper. Gnomes with mushrooms are a common ANRI theme. $75-95.

In 1948, ANRI introduced a line of stopper holders, or stands, from the original designs by Eduard Mahlknecht. They were very popular and came in a variety of styles. Many were painted and carved to look like fences painted with trees and flowers.

These stands were available with up to twelve holes to accommodate a large assortment of stoppers and were sold with or without corks. Watch for racks with entire lower bodies painted on them, so that when the stoppers are in place, they form a complete human form. These racks were retired from production in 1958. Racks without stoppers, $25-75.

Once ANRI became a major exporter to fine gift shops around the world, they began to produce special display racks for bottle stoppers that were provided to retailers with their orders. Racks without stoppers, $40-50.

Wholesale catalog pages from the 1950s show ANRI racks and a variety of stoppers produced at the time for retail shops and souvenir stores in many countries. It's interesting to see the price for a dozen bottle stoppers at that time. A single bottle stopper retailed for about $2.50 in the early 1970s.

In the following pages we present an ANRI bottle stopper gallery featuring displays from several collectors. Stoppers that were not produced by ANRI are noted. Once you have become familiar with most models and have a basic understanding of how they work, the variety of possibilities shown here should encourage you to continue the search for additions to your own collection. We hope both seasoned and beginning collectors find new inspiration, so enjoy the show!

A group of "blinking" stoppers.

A mixed collection of stoppers and pourers. Some nice older models can be seen on both rows.

The two on the right are very early and unusual bottle stoppers with stem bases.

On the stopper, second from the left, note the interesting combination of carving and painting to indicate eyeglasses.

It is unlikely that the older lady with her hair in a bun or the man with the black mustache were produced by ANRI

This photograph shows a long bottle stopper display stand with fence design.

Here is a fine group of hat tippers and drinkers, including one with a headscarf on the left. On the right is an example of the earlier carved eyeglasses.

The middle row on this rack shows a set of Dickens character stoppers. They are, from the left, the Artful Dodger, Dolly Varden, Mr. Macawber, Sarah Gamp, David Copperfield, Mr. Dick, Joe the Fat Boy, Mr. Pecksniff, Mr. Pickwick, Sam Weller, Captain Cuttle, and Job. Trotter.

In the top row a series of four large bird stopper/pourers are a rooster, an eagle or hawk, a parrot, and a bird of paradise. Pourers are covered in the next chapter of this book.

The bottom row has several hard to find items. Just to the right of the acrobat monkey is a stopper that depicts eggs in a basket. Instead of a regular cork, it has a rubber sleeve which serves to seal the bottle when this stopper is in place. This kind of bottle stopper was produced in the late 1930s and few survived due to the deterioration of the rubber.

To the right of the egg basket is a small, carved doll in a fabric dress. These dolls were also used on pincushions, trinket boxes, and sold separately in several sizes during the very early 1900s.

On the left end of the bottom row is a "reading mule" that has lost his book. On both rows there are several stoppers with original fabric scarves and ties.

The three tall stoppers are very early ANRI models that are pictured in trade catalogs from the late 1920s.

The red and green carved wooden flower positioned in the middle of this rack was not produced by ANRI.

The lady on the left wasn't produced by the carvers at ANRI. It has a lever that lowers the top of her blue swimsuit. The bird and the caricature of Sir Winston Churchill are very early ANRI stoppers.

The Santa Claus stopper is a "head in head" with a small head revealed when the cap is up.

This photograph shows a wonderful group of ethnic and character stoppers and one Black corkscrew.

On the bottom row the "Old Crow" bottle stopper may have been produced as an advertising piece for the Old Crow Distillery, Frankfort, Kentucky. The mouse, with a movable bead/neck, second from the right, is another in the "dressed animals" series that was produced before the mid-1920s.

ANRI caricatures of locals from the Gröden Valley were also sold as figurines and added to other items.

A nice group of dogs including "Bottoms-up" and "Your Health" toasts.

This unusual group contains a man with a patch on one eye (far left) and two less common stopper/pourers with small animals atop wooden bases (far right). The two cats are the same models that may be found in various bar sets, which were also sold separately.

These larger stoppers with unusually large corks were produced by ANRI. $200-250.

ANRI bears may be found engaged in a variety of activities including kissing, drinking, and playing musical instruments.

What would you give for this enti rack of special stoppers?

Notice the th gnomes with b wooden feet sitti on top of barre Two stopp pourers are weari bright green tuni and one bot stopper is in yello They were p duced in the m 192

The Winston Churchill carving, fifth from the left, is a pourer with a nickel-plated collar

The first two stoppers from the left are nice examples of the two-faced hat flipper model. The reading man, second from the right, is the oldest and most well carved example found to date. He is also a blinker.

'here are so many great stoppers in this rack it's hard to know which one to look ι first. The first two on the left have the inserted, wooden peg noses. The fourth ɾom the left has the two-piece head that wobbles (covered later in the bar set ection). The monk carved in full figure and the Pope in papal robes with metallic old painted details are very hard to find.

The stopper on the left is very unusual with the wooden peg nose and a face on each side of the head.

The fourth stopper from the right is a simple push puppet holding a little carved guitar. Second from the left is a clown with wine bottles on strings in each hand.

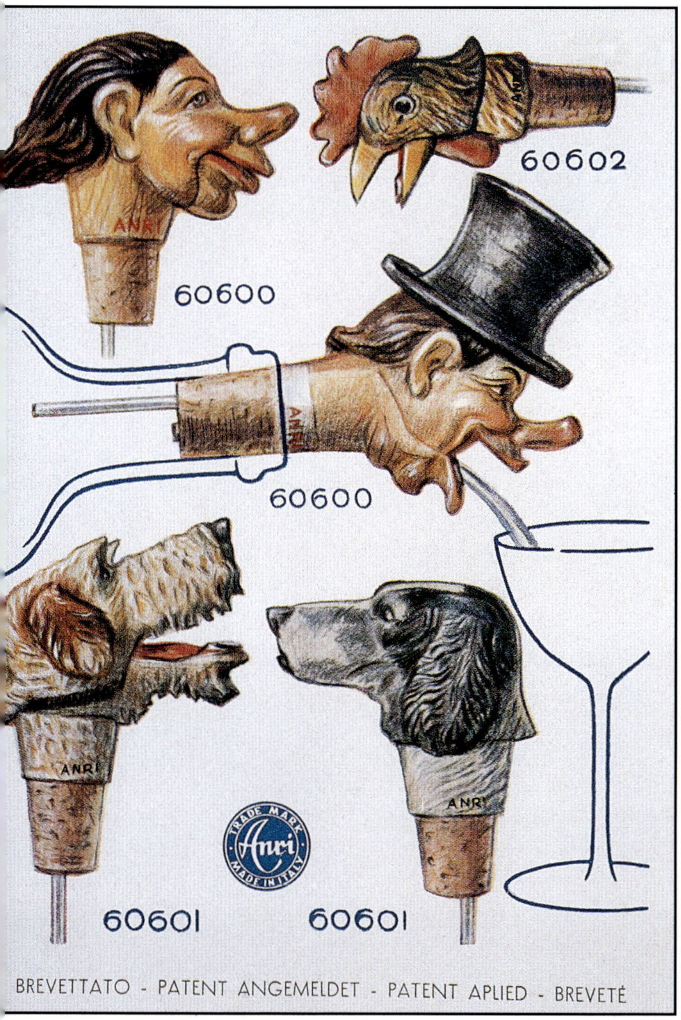

A "pourer" seals a bottle but also dispenses the beverage inside. The cork stopper seals it and a tube that extends through the cork into the bottle allows the wine or liquor to flow out. ANRI made hundreds of different pouring stoppers. Some were very simple while others were elaborate with detailed carving, but all appeal to collectors.

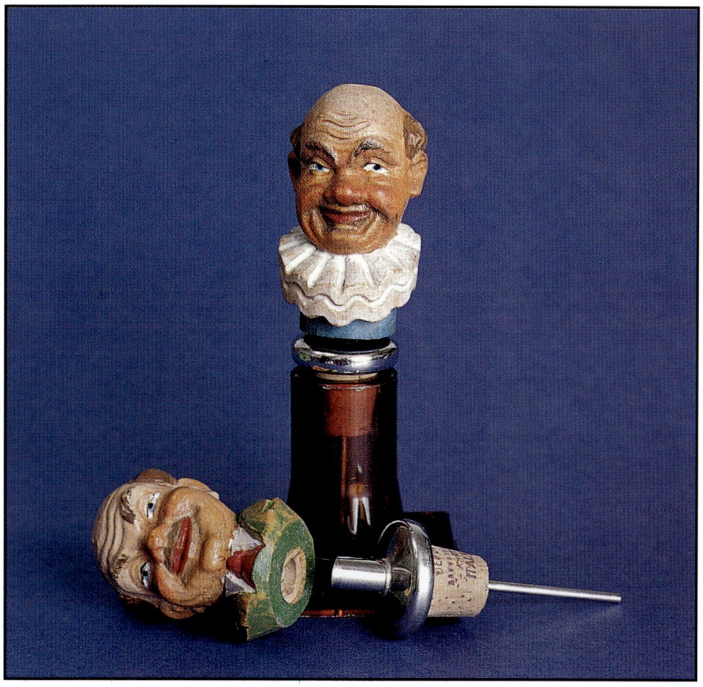

This type of pourer has a carved wooden head atop a nickel-plated tube and collar. The tube isn't visible until the head is removed, exposing the small spout beneath. Pictured are two very fine examples of the larger head carvings, a clown and a man in native attire. 2.5" tall. $75-95.

Three more large pourers with metal collars and tubes, including a cook. The fourth carving (on the right) is not a pourer. $75-95.

These three pourers also require removal of the carvings but the collars on those to the left and right are wood instead of metal. The word "Depose" can be seen stamped or carved into the collars, which is French for "Patented." These are 3" to 3.5" tall from collar to top of head. The smaller one is 1.5" tall. Large, $40-55. Small, $30-45.

Many examples of this style pourer were produced. $35-45.

Some pourers have brightly colored plastic pouring tubes and collars. $35-45.

These pourers don't require removing the carved top from the cork. They were designed so that when the pourer is tipped forward, the bottom jaw drops down, exposing the built in spout. Of this type, two lady characters may be found: one is carved and painted so that both eyes are looking toward her right, while the other seems to be winking her left eye. The gentlemen pourers of this model are commonly called, "Mortimer Snerd," because of their resemblance to a ventriloquist dummy used by Edgar Bergen in the 1930s. $65-85.

Here are happy faces in a variety of different hats. The pourer on the right has a rubber tube protruding from his mouth, which is the pour spout that doubles as a cigar. $65-85.

This model, some of which resemble the film star, W. C. Fields, has the addition of a built in Swiss music box. Musical movements were added to ANRI bar items in the 1950s. Sizes range from 3.25" to 4" as measured from collar to top of hat. Tipping the stopper causes the music to begin and it stops when the bottle is brought back to an upright position. In mint condition, the music box should stop and start as designed. Unfortunately, many of these have been over wound and no longer play. A variety of tunes may be found including "How Dry I Am," as well as traditional German and Italian drinking songs and waltzes. Also, watch for musical clowns and a fish with applied fabric fins, made of felt. $65-85. MIB, $75-100.

These larger pourers are three-fourths of a quartet of birds ANRI produced in the early 1950s that included a rooster, a Bird of Paradise, a hawk or eagle, and a parrot. The parrot and rooster are brightly painted, while the hawk and Bird of Paradise have only minimal coloration. These range in size from 3" to 4", collar to top. The pour spout is revealed with the opening of the beak. $75-90.

Smaller, but just as charming, are the ANRI pourers depicting various dog breeds. These also have the pour spout inside the mouth with a movable lower jaw and range from 2.5" to 3.5" tall from collar to top. $60-85.

Some pourers have the metal tube protruding from the mouth. Small pourers measuring approximately 1.5" can be found. $40-60.

Three canine pourers: a white Scottie, a setter, and a Saint Bernard. $45-65.

ANRI also produced mechanical pouring stoppers with full figure carvings. This fellow straddling a big wine bottle is slightly over 4" tall from base to top. ANRI catalogs advertised him as "Lacky Pourer." To pour, press down on his coattail and he uncaps the bottle, revealing the spout. $85-95.

ANRI called this pourer "Barrel Stunts." It features a man sitting on a barrel with his legs dangling over the front. When the bot is tilted to pour, he swings up and away a somersault motion exposing the metal spout. 4.5" from base to top of head. $85-9

This model is called "Emptying the Barrel" and has a built-in Swiss music box. The man is draped over a beer barrel with his hand on the spigot. When the pourer is tilted forward, the man's right hand swings away exposing the spout, and the music plays. 4" tall, 1.5" deep, and 3" wide measured without the cork. $100-125.

Bottle Openers & Corkscrews

Two accessories no bartender or host can survive without are a corkscrew for opening bottles of wine and a cap lifter for opening bottles of ale. ANRI produced both in abundance. You may find the opener or corkscrew inserted into the carved heads of people or animals, as the removable part of full figure carvings, or as singles. Values in this category vary with age and subject matter.

Based on the style of the metal insert, the oldest of this group is the man second from the right. These pieces measure from 2" to 3.5" tall excluding the metal opener. $45-75.

As seen here, not all bottle openers were painted. Some were left natural. $45-60.

The second important tool for the bar is the corkscrew and ANRI made hundreds of models. $50-75.

American Indians, now called Native Americans, also served as handles for corkscrews. $70-85.

There were many kinds of animal carvings, like the llama and dogs shown. $70-85.

This Negro woman is an excellent model of early ANRI corkscrew and was made in the 1920s. $75-85.

Two terrier corkscrews. $55-65.

When a human figure corkscrew or bottle stopper is found with the carving ending at the neck rather than continuing into the shoulder/waistline area, it was probably made to be included in a bar set or inserted into a carved wooden body. If you have sets with missing parts, it's a smart idea to look for tools like this one to use as replacements.

Single corkscrews of Gröden Valley characters, some older than others, but all wonderful.

A fun quest for collectors is searching for a canine bottle opener and cap lifter of the same breed to make a set. $55-65.

This bottle opener and corkscrew are two elements from the "Cannibal" revolving bar set ANRI issued in 1953-54. The set had three figures in native African dress including a bottle stopper and a ballerina figure that twirled in the center of a drum. A complete Cannibal bar set is very hard to find. Single elements, $45-65. Complete set, $175-200.

This very unusual item has a corkscrew on one end and a cap lifter on the other. $100.

Many corkscrews and bottle openers were produced with fully carved figural stands. This Skye terrier stands 5" tall and the head lifts off to reveal the worm. $75-95.

This amusing corkscrew is a squirrel that rests within a base carved to look like a tree stump decorated with mushrooms. 5" overall. $75-85.

This jaunty fellow does something quite different. When his head is turned, his arms rise. The worm is attached at waist level and the corkscrew rests inside the carved lower body. 7" tall. $100.

These are examples of finely carved bottle openers and corkscrews with figural holders or stands. $75-90.

The stands on these bar tools contain Swiss music boxes that play when the heads are removed. The corkscrew on the left plays "When Irish Eyes Are Smiling" and the bottle opener on the right plays "Marinella." $95-125.

ANRI produced lots of monks and these are some great examples. Single figural stands range in size from 5.5" to 7". $75-90.

The three monks on the left contain cap lifters and the three on the right are cork-screws. $75-90.

The monk in the center is holding a snuffbox and to his right is a knitting monk. $75-90.

It is more common to find bar tool figures carved to resemble the ordinary people and attire from the Tyrol region. It is interesting to note that no single, free standing, fully carved female bar tools have been seen. Careful study of these figures should help you distinguish the differences between ANRI carvings and those produced elsewhere. $75-85.

As you can see, there are literally endless variations to costume and facial carving so there is no limit to the number of pieces you may add to your collection. In most cases the heads and bodies are interchangeable, so don't be afraid to buy less than perfect items. They can be replaced with time and patience. $75-85.

A bar set, as defined in this book, is an ANRI model containing more than one bar tool. Some of the bar sets from ANRI have only one figure but incorporate several items in their design, making them useful for a greater number of tasks. Bar sets may have a corkscrew, a bottle opener, a bottle stopper, or coasters, in any combination.

This stunning Negro waiter is seen holding three huge mugs of beer, and carrying a bar towel over his left arm. The head is a corkscrew, the "beer foam" on top of the mugs are bottle stoppers, and the bar towel is a cap lifter. It is also one of the taller pieces, measuring 10" tall. $400-450.

This type of bar set may be found in a variety of sizes, with and without "beer foam" bottle stoppers, as in the small figures on the right and left. The middle waiter is 10.5" tall and is mounted on a 4.5" x 4.5" base. His head is a corkscrew. $200-250. The waiter on the left is 7.5" tall and conceals a cap lifter, while the small one on the right stands 5.5" tall. Lifting his head reveals a simple bottle cork. $75-100.

Large bar set with corkscrew. 10" tall. $80-100.

These three examples represent the difference in facial features when a figure is meant to be a caricature, as in the figures on the left and in the center vs. a realistic, portrait type carving like the one on the right. As an added delight, the figure on the left has a Swiss music box concealed inside. 7" to 7.5" tall with base. $75-100.

The tall figure on the right contains a music box. $80-100.

Here is another type of ANRI bar set with three bar tools behind a fence-stand. As in the stopper sets, the tools are inserted into slots behind the fence. Most sets of three contain a bottle stopper, a corkscrew, and a bottle opener. 5" to 7" wide. $75-90.

This four-piece set contains an extra bottle stopper. Notice the second figure from the left, a man with a scarf tied around his head beneath a hat. Several ANRI bottle stoppers and other carvings show this type of "head dress." One wonders if this was the old fashioned way to keep ears warm on cold windy days or if the character is suffering from a toothache. He refuses to say. $75-95.

This combination key rack and bar set is designed to stand alone or hang on a wall. Carved with articulated legs attached to the stand, the bar tools complete the figures. They are, from the left, a bottle opener, a corkscrew, and a bottle stopper. There is also one key hook left of the original four. 9.5" wide, 1.5" deep. $95-125.

This particular set is one of the oldest models ANRI produced. Notice the care taken with the painting of the flowers on the fence, but the real treasures are the bar tools. The wide-open mouths and carved tongues are obvious but the clever design can't be seen in a printed photograph. The carved tongues and bodies are of one piece of wood, while the carved heads are another. The two pieces are attached in the way of conventional "nodders," so that the heads wobble back and forth making the tongues seem to protrude and withdraw. $175-200.

In 1950, when Guilio Sestini joined ANRI, the line of bar sets and accessories expanded including larger sets in which people and animals were used. This Sestini design, issued in 1953-54, is the one most commonly found: a man holding both arms open wide with oversized shoes providing a resting place for a set of painted coasters. Different objects are seen in the hands: mugs, steins, bottles, and even turnips. The head in this model is usually attached to a bottle opener. $65-80.

This style of coaster set is approximately 6" to 6.5" tall. Original coasters, like the ones pictured, are difficult to come by. The head in this type is usually attached to a bottle opener. The sailor is an exception having a can piercer attached. Without coasters, $65-80. With original coasters, $85-125.

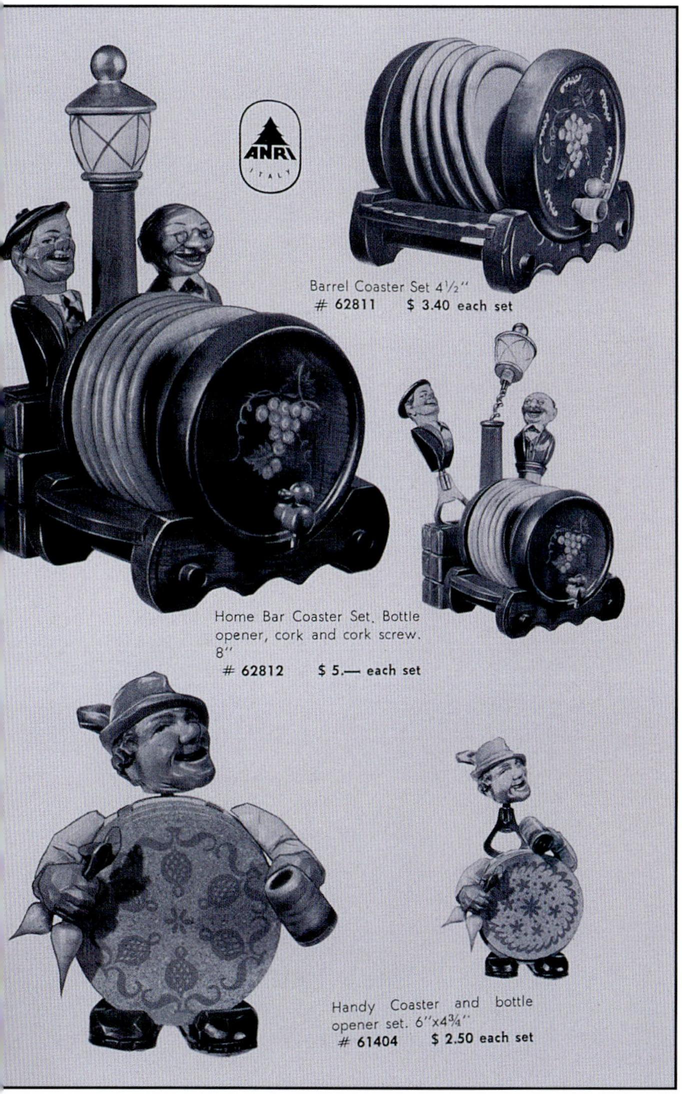

This page from a 1950s catalog shows other coaster stands and sets including corkscrews, bottle openers, and the occasional stopper. The prices shown are wholesale.

Coaster stand with standing figures, which conceal a bottle opener and corkscrew. $90.

Coaster stand with a sailor having a bottle opener head and a concertina. 6.25" wide and 5.5" tall. $95.

An Alpine man peeking around a stein holds a set of coasters and has a corkscrew attached to the beer foam. 5.5" tall by 5.5" wide. $100.

Dubbed the "Happy Monk" in old ANRI catalogs, but called the "Monk On Barrel" by collectors, this bar piece is a staple for every collection. It consists of a monk, or other figure, sitting on top of a barrel with one or more additional implements behind. The set is most often found in the 5.5" to 6" size, but taller barrels over 7" tall were made and usually have a built in music box. Without music, $65-75. With music, $75-85.

Monks may have brightly painted aprons over plain brown robes or the colors may be muted and pale. The removable heads are corkscrews. Behind the figures you may find the addition of a bottle opener in the form of a wine bottle, and on some sets, a mug of beer with a bottle stopper of foam. $65-75. The two tall barrels contain music boxes. $75-85.

Much more difficult to find are sailors on barrels with and without bottle opener/wine bottles. The standing sailor conceals a corkscrew. Standing Sailor, $85. Sailors on Barrels, $75-90.

These people seem to be hiding in their barrels. Some are bottle openers and others are corkscrews. $55-65.

The "Drunk on a Lamppost" is easy to find. He's a tipsy man with a cigar in his right hand standing under a streetlight. It typically measures 10" from the top of the lamp to the bottom of the base, but there are many differences from piece to piece, as seen in the following photographs. Along with the variations in clothing and hats, different faces and light globes atop the poles offer the collector an opportunity to vary his collection many ways. The head is usually a bottle opener with the lamp being a corkscrew. $75-85.

Behind these two "Drunks on a Lampposts" are suitcases, which are music boxes. $85-100.

Another variation is a dog standing on the base with the man. On the right a man in what looks like a "Zoot" suit stands with a large French poodle. It is unusual, too, that he is leaning on the opposite side of the post, and both the lamp and the poodle's head contain corkscrews. His head is a traditional bottle opener. $85-100.

These drunks have pet dogs. $75-85.

Both of these are musical. The one on the left is mounted on a round music box.

This set has a sleeping dog and a sober looking man holding a hat in his left hand. This man's head is a corkscrew and this lamp does not have a removable globe. The dog is made of plaster and may not be original to the piece. $125.

Left: The sailor playing a concertina is a cap lifter and the lamp is a corkscrew. $95.

Right: Another unusual type has a recessed area to one side of the lamppost, which serves as a resting place for a bottle of wine. $85-95.

These guys aren't drunks, they're just hanging out, sitting on a wall under a lamppost. The lamp atop the pole is the corkscrew, one man is a bottle opener, and the other man is a bottle stopper. 8.5" tall to top of lamp. $85-95.

This Sestini set varies in clothing, hats, and facial features. The two gentlemen have articulated lower bodies and it is interesting to note their legs which are sometimes carved with ankles crossed, one leg over the other, or hanging straight. $85-95.

Bottom left: The figure on the right is often carved carrying a bottle in his left hand. When the heads are removed you have a bottle opener and a corkscrew for your home bar. They stand 7" tall from top of hat to bottom of base. $85-95.

Bottom right: Another model that offers an endless variety of combinations is the "Buddy Set" with two friends arm in arm. Are they out for a walk or has one of them had too much to drink at the local pub and needs the steadying hand of his pal? The heads are a bottle stopper and a corkscrew. $80-90.

Three partying pairs. $65-75.

This set is from the 1950s, evidenced by the brighter colored clothing and less realistic carving. $65-75.

Seen here, a different type of two man set containing a bottle opener and a corkscrew, but instead of being carved of one piece of wood, they are separate figures on one base. $65-80.

We can only guess at what ANRI was trying to tell us with this set. People used to say that a drunk was, "In his cups." These guys are totally in their bottles. The men in the barrels are bottle openers and the corkscrews are in the bottles. 6" wide, 2" deep, and over 7" tall. $70-$85.

This less common bar set has both a man bottle opener and a woman corkscrew. 8.5" tall, 7.75" wide, and 4" deep. $85.

A very unusual two-character set features a circus clown and a trained seal. Even more unusual is that the clown's head is attached to a can opener. The ball on the seal's nose is a corkscrew. 8" wide, 8" tall, and 3.25" deep. $125.

First you take a simple park bench, then add a couple of guys sitting around with nothing to do except help you open bottles. That's the "Men on Benches" bar set, another Sestini design from the 1950s.

As you can see, there's no set rule about which man is the corkscrew and which is the bottle opener. The metal elements were not specific to either figure. The characters in this set always seem to be unhappy with each other, usually sitting back to back, but poses differ. 6" tall, by 6" wide. $65-80.

Note that this set has a different look than the others. Issued in 1959, these figures were designed by Guilio Sestini. Without the bright colors of the others, they were made in natural wood with minimal painted detail. Sestini also designed a drunk on a lamppost, a two man set with a singer and a guitar player, a man leaning on a barrel which opened to hold cigarettes, and a man lounging on top of a keg with a bottle across his lap. Sestini creations are easy to identify due to their angular faces and the use of fine hardwoods. These Sestini bar sets were retired in 1962. In 1961, the two-man set on the nicer park bench retailed for $17.50. $70-85.

The three-piece set has the addition of a cork stopper cat. Cats may be seen in a variety of colors and although some seem quite friendly, others were carved with flattened ears and arched backs probably from being put too close to dog carvings. 7" wide by 6.5" tall. 3 piece set, $85-95.

In this two-piece set, a man seems to be drinking his lunch while he rests on top of a picnic table or small bench. Posed on top of the beer barrel, to the right, are cats that serve as corkscrews. 4.25" wide and 6" tall. $65-75.

One would expect this model with three figures to contain at least two, if not three, separate bar tools but this is another ANRI surprise. For all its detail and the amusing addition of a drinking monkey on top of the keg, only the man on the right of each picnic table is a bar tool. Two of these sets have combination corkscrew / cap lifters and one has a tin or can opener. 7.75" wide by 5.5" tall. $75-90.

Three men and a guitar compose the "Musical Trio" bar set, but as with all ANRI carvings, no two are exactly alike. $85-95.

Typically, the center man is the musician holding a guitar or a stringed instrument resembling a mandolin. His two partners stand on either side but not all partners sing. Some are just happy standing by. As in many ANRI bar sets, the large suitcase behind the trio on the right conceals a wind up music box. All trios include a bottle stopper, a corkscrew, and a cap lifter. $75-95.

This model is 7" wide and 7" tall and the quality of carving and detail varies. These two sets were produced in the 1930s or 1940s. $75-95.

More trios. $75-95.

Two man musical sets are less common. The one on the left was retired in 1962, along with the other Sestini designs. 8.75" tall and according to the caption in a 1959 ANRI catalog it was carved of "finest hardwoods." $80-90.

It is also possible to discover the musical trio bar set with Sailor figures. These are more difficult to find and coveted by collectors who must compete with those who collect nautical items. In the first set, each figure has an applied sticker reading "Stratheden" on the brims of their caps. Two are visible in this photograph, but on the right the sticker is in back. The *Stratheden* was a British passenger ship launched in1937, that served as a troop transport in 1939. In the 1950s it sailed from Southampton to New York under Cunard charter. The second set is from the *Montclare*, a Canadian ship that operated from 1922 until 1958. It was a pleasure cruiser in the 1930s and was sold to the British Admiralty in 1942. These bar sets were exported by ANRI and sold as souvenirs. 7.75" wide and 7" tall. $350+.

Single musician bar tools were also produced like this man with a guitar. His head is a corkscrew. $45-60.

Some ANRI bar sets incorporated vehicles like this two-man model with a trunk full of coasters. The removable heads are a corkscrew and a bottle opener. $75-90.

This set is pictured in a 1956 ANRI catalog and features a whimsical horse drawn carriage with a driver and three passengers. The visitors are carved in caricature to resemble Japanese tourists. A similar set was produced with the same four figures in a convertible touring car, which was carved in side view with the figures along side each other. In both models the driver is a corkscrew, the front passenger is a bottle opener, and backseat passengers are bottle stoppers. The carriage is 8" tall by 4" deep and 7" wide at the lanterns. It has the number 13 painted on the back. $100.

A bar scene differs from a bar set due to the wooden frame, or walls, surrounding the figures. ANRI produced several of these scenes or dioramas. Many were never pictured in any catalog. Men and women in the Gröden Valley, monks, animals, and other figures were used. All include a corkscrew, bottle opener, and at least one bottle stopper. The designs originated with Guilio Sestini and were issued in the 1950s.

One bar scene that is relatively easy to find is the "Monks In a Wine Cellar." It contains three figures in brown robes gathered around a large wine cask. $200-225.

The Monks in the Wine Cellar scene was produced with and without a music box as shown on this 1950s era ANRI catalog p .ge. The monks' poses vary, as do the variety of small elements on the shelf and floor. Some have different painted details such as brick or stone designs on the walls and floor. The removable heads are a corkscrew, bottle opener, and stopper. $200-225. Also pictured on the catalog page is the bar set with two men sitting on a wall. The prices on the catalog page are wholesale.

This unusual scene featuring a single monk with a wine bottle in each hand was issued in the late 1950s and illustrated in an ANRI catalog in 1959. On either side of the figure are four wine casks. In this model the monk is a solid carving without a removable head. The two top barrels remove and are a corkscrew and bottle opener. The original wholesale price for the set was $7.50. It measures 8.75" wide, 3.25" deep, and 6" tall. Single Monk Bar Scene, $175-200.

Another large Sestini designed scene is the "Beer Bar" depicting a traditional pub with a bartender, three patrons on barstools, and a standing figure with a musical instrument. The head of the bartender is a corkscrew, his customers are bottle stoppers, and the musician hides a bottle opener. Scattered about the shelves and bar counter are little wooden bottles and mugs attached to cocktail toothpicks. This model is 12" wide, 8" deep, and 9.5" tall. This was produced by ANRI with and without a Swiss music box. Those with the wind up music boxes have an added surprise. When the corkscrew head is removed, the music plays as the bartender moves his arm up and down tapping a mug of beer on the bar. Originals had a mirrored back bar. Without music, $250-300. Musical, $275-350.

As seen in this reproduction of a catalog page from the late 1950s, the "beer bar" originally sold at wholesale for $8 without music and $12.50 with music box and movement. Many are found with the ANRI 40th Anniversary sticker from 1952 and production of this item spanned several years. It is also important to note that in early sets the musician was a man in Tyrolean dress. The sailor figure appeared in later models.

In the "Amor Bar" we see the addition of a tiny ballerina in the middle of the table. "Amor" was designed with a built in Swiss music box and while the music plays, the ballerina twirls and dances. This Sestini design was introduced in 1953-54. Astute collectors know that the lamppost hides a corkscrew attached to the globe, as in other bar sets, and the customers around the table contain bottle stoppers. The standing waiter's head is a bottle opener. In mint condition with working ballerina and music box, $275-300.

ANRI called this smaller bar scene "Separe Bar." It contains two seated figures, a tabletop ballerina, and a dog. This set measures 6" wide and has a traditional red and white-checkered fabric tablecloth. The ballerina means this set was also equipped with a Swiss music box and she bobs up and down, and twirls while it plays. The figures' poses and breeds of dog vary. Again, the globe of the lamp is a corkscrew and the customers are a bottle stopper and opener. With working music box and ballerina, $175-200.

Another wine cellar diorama is this model with a series of barrels, three characters, and a cat. This particular piece is thought to be in its original condition as produced in the early 1950s. The cat is a corkscrew and the two men inside the large upright barrels are bottle stoppers. The sleeping figure sitting on the floor pulls out and is the bottle opener. The small barrel on the right was designed to hold toothpicks. This bar scene has a working Swiss music box and a fully functional ballerina dancing atop the barrel of 1905 vintage wine. $300-350.

ANRI produced two additional bar scenes in the 1950s that are not pictured. The "Moulin Rouge" had two gentlemen seated in front of a house façade, a standing waiter, a dancing ballerina, and a cat corkscrew atop the roof. It also incorporated a Swiss music box. $175-200. The "Crazy Moon" bar had a lady on a balcony, a man playing a guitar behind a wall on the right, and sleeping man bottle opener on the left. The painted back wall depicted whimsical buildings silhouetted against a smiling full moon. Each was 8" wide, 3" deep, and 10" tall. $150-200.

Another example of this bar scene model has basically the same elements but the bottle stopper lady holding a rolling pin is not original to the set. 8.5" wide by 7" deep and 8.5" tall. Both models have the number 1905 painted on the front of the center barrel just above the spigot. This does not denote the year this scene was produced, but it was listed as such by Christie's Auction House, London, when the first of the two sets shown here was offered during a corkscrew auction in the late 1990s. $300-350.

ANRI made many items that were never pictured in their catalogs but are some of the finest things they ever produced. One example is the "Sweet Adeline" bar scene, so named because originally the sign read, "Next Number Sweet Adeline." The word is spelled "Adoline" on some signs. The scene has a bar with a brass rail, a bartender, and three gentlemen with their mouths open in song. The bartender makes the fourth in the quartet and is a bottle opener. Some have been found with a late 1920s ANRI paper label but since the label design didn't change until 1950, it is impossible to know exactly when it was produced. The Sweet Adeline bar scene is 12" long by 4.25" deep. The bar is 4.5" tall. $300-350.

The "Old Soak" bar scene, so called because of the name painted across the bar, has many of the same features as the "Sweet Adeline." The bar and brass rail are similar and the bartender has a familiar face. But, just in case this isn't the kind of place where "everybody knows your name," the four patron bottle stoppers on bar "spools" have their names painted on just above their corks. They are, from the left, "Ole Tom," "Harry the Duke," "Ole Jake," and "Ole Kate." The bartenders are a corkscrew and a bottle opener. This model is also the largest of ANRI's bar scenes, 12" long by 4.5" deep. The bar is 4.5" high and the stools are 3" tall. Overall the piece is 7" tall at the highest point. $300-375.

A closer view of some of the "Old Soak regulars" gives a better idea of what to look for as you search. Note the color and detail differences. These were found without the bar so perhaps there is an abandoned bar stool somewhere just waiting to be found. $65-70.

One of the most rare and desirable bar scenes ANRI produced depicts the "The Cotton Club," a famous Negro nightclub. The sign is faded and barely legible from age, but it reads "Cotton Club Members Only." The two men seated at the table are bottle stoppers; the man standing and dressed in pale blue is a corkscrew.

There is one implement missing from the scene pictured. A slot behind the far wall originally held a Negro woman bottle opener but, sadly, she has been lost. A series of small wooden pieces on top of the table form a radio with a round disk representing the speaker.

Two other "Cotton Club "scenes have been found with bottle openers intact but with slightly different figures. Both had missing signs and one had lost parts of the table radio. To date, none has been found in mint condition, so keep looking. 10.25" wide, 4" deep, and 8.5" tall at the top of the sign. $1000-1500.

ANRI produced a variety of bar accessories other than the stoppers and tools seen thus far, but few like this one. This simple unadorned wooden bar tray with a raised lip measures 12.5" long and 7.75" wide. On the handles are two 4.5" tall men carved in full figure. One man holds a mug and the other plays a concertina. Both have removable heads, one a bottle opener and the other a corkscrew. $450.

Age and household cooking or heating smoke has blackened this old ANRI bottle holder, but some of her original color is still visible. By twisting the top and bottom in opposite directions, the body separates in the middle and the hollow figure accommodates a bottle of wine. Recessed inside the head there is a cork for capping the bottle. 10.75" tall. In original condition, $225-250.

Keep your eyes open for ANRI cocktail picks. These little guys have carved and painted faces with a variety of expressions. They measure about 4" long and were originally sold by the dozen. Each, $15-20.

These muddlers were produced by ANRI before 1950. On some of them the bottoms are scored for crushing garnishes or pieces of citrus fruit added to mixed drinks. Lengths vary for glasses of different sizes. $45-65.

This photograph is a small collection of items featuring the same cheerful face most often seen in ANRI bar sets and scenes as the bartender. The smallest item (right foreground) is a place card holder.

Part Four

ANRI Figurines

ANRI has been making figurines since the early 20th Century and they are still producing Limited Edition figurines. ANRI trade catalog #4 from1925 pictured twenty-four pages of decorative figures and literally hundreds were shown. Even more were added through the 1940s.

Collectors may find Gröden Valley folk in native costumes, musicians, monks, religious figures, and animals. Later, figures depicting Doctors and other professions were added.

The most common indication that a figurine was produced by ANRI is the shape of the wooden base. The vast majority of them are octagonal, an almost square block of wood with the four corners carved away at an angle. But, not all ANRI bases have this shape, so while this is helpful in the identification process, it is not a foolproof method. Some of their figurines were carved with round or simple square bases.

The ANRI carvers used each other as models. Their carvings depicted Gröden Valley people going about their day-to-day routines dressed in native clothing like the woman with the rake shown here. Their value is found, not just in the beauty of the art itself but from an historic aspect, these early ANRI carvings have preserved the people of the Tyrol and their daily lives for posterity.

These two figures showing a man on his way to market with a small pig under his arm and a woman with her basket of eggs are 12.25" tall. They were produced from 1912 until the early 1920s. One indication of their age is their large size and the thickness of the bases on which they stand. $95-125.

These ladies are sweeping or on the way to market with chickens. Or perhaps they are on their way back? They range in size from 3.5" to 8" tall. $45-75.

All of these ladies are knitting and some of the knitting needles are metal. They range from 3" to 8" tall. $35-85.

This group illustrates the great variety of models ANRI produced. 5" to 8.25" tall. $55-85.

This group is 3.25" to 6" tall.

Not all statuettes of the Gröden Valley ladies depict them doing housework or chores. The figures on the left and right show more formal or holiday attire. 5" to 8" tall. $55-75.

One indication of the age of ANRI figurines is the thickness of the bases on which they stand. Older carvings have taller bases and the Cembra pine from which they were carved has darkened with age. 7" to 7.25" tall. $65-85.

Fewer female than male figurines were made in all categories but those that do exist are charming. The smallest in this group is only 1.5" tall including the base. The tallest is 4.25". $45-85.

The men of northern Italy were well represented by the ANRI Master carvers. This gentleman in his apron might have been a carpenter or another kind of laborer and is shown holding a coin. 10" tall. $85.

The man on the left is seen in a pose used in many ANRI carvings: hands in pockets and legs widely spaced. The man on the right is probably a caricature of some silent film star or cartoon character from the early 1920s but his identity remains a mystery. 7.5" tall. $65-100.

These figures were produced consistently from the 1920s through the late 1950s. One chap is playing Bocce ball while his neighbor to the right is polishing his boot (notice one of his feet is bare). The two with lanterns are night watchmen. These are 7" to 9" tall. $90-95.

This foursome was produced from the early 1920s through the late 1940s. The tallest is over 12". The music teacher is missing the baton for his right hand. $95-125.

The man with the red umbrella is 12.25" tall. The lady figurine is missing a cane in her right hand but is unusual because of the prayer book and rosary in her left one. She is 8" tall. When viewed from the back, the barefoot man has his shoes tied together and hanging over one shoulder. 12" tall. $95-125.

Men holding umbrellas over their heads are not as common as those holding closed ones in their hands or under one arm. The figures with umbrellas open are 5" tall. The big guy is 10" tall. $75-85.

With majestic mountains like the Dolomites and Alps nearby, it's only natural that the ANRI carvers produced figurines depicting hikers and mountain climbers. The smallest is only 3" tall and the largest is 10". $45-85.

Another common theme is this man smoking a long stemmed pipe. These range from 4" to 10" tall. Sadly, some of them have lost their delicate pipe stems. $45-85.

Men going to market. 2.5" to 7" tall. $35-75.

These men look quite pleased with themselves, carved with their hands in pockets and legs far apart. This pose is another one that was carved consistently from the early 1920s through the late 1950s. $45-85.

This group includes some less common figures as well as some familiar faces. The man with the blue scarf and his neighbor with the purple scarf are more caricature carvings than realistic, portrait types. 4.5" to 8" tall. $65-85.

Hunting was an important part of life in the Gröden Valley and ANRI produced some wonderful figurines of huntsmen. The large hunter with a gun is 10" tall. The man with a deer over his shoulders is a less common model and a similar one is shown in an ANRI trade catalog from 1921. $75-100.

This figurine of a traveling clock salesman is quite unique and was produced in the mid-1920s. $130.

The bootblack is shining his own boot and the blacksmith, standing in front of an anvil, holds an infant. $65-100.

Notice the man in the center with the red umbrella. He is looking down at a tiny frog carved onto the base. Must have been quite a rainstorm. $55-100.

These figures are 4" to 8" tall. $55-85.

These familiar figures range from 3.25" to 5.25" tall. $55-75.

Oppposite page, top: Another couples theme is this seated man and woman shown sharing a newspaper. Both women in this pair of figurines are knitting. 5" and 7" tall. $95-120.

Bottom: Here is another group of couples sharing the morning paper but the figurine on the right has been damaged. A previous owner remembered playing with these carvings as a child. They were brought to the US by his grandparents from Austria before the early 1920s. 5" to 7" tall. $100-120.

This trio of gentlemen is from the very early 1900s and have the neck/bead feature that makes their heads movable. The detailed carving of their facial expressions is especially well done. 7.5" tall. $100-150.

ANRI carvers didn't just produce single figures of men and women. Some very wonderful figurines were made of couples like this one of a man and woman dancing. This photograph shows two sides of a single carving. This model was made in three sizes, 7", 12", and 14" tall It is pictured in trade catalogs from 1912. The one shown is 7" tall. $150-175.

Anton Riffeser, the founder of ANRI, probably created the master carvings for the figurines shown here. Similar carvings stand in the Val Gardena Museum in St. Ulrich/Ortisei, Italy, just a few miles from the ANRI studios. Since Anton Riffeser and his fellow soldiers were held captive in Siberia during WWI and used Russian peasants as their models, the carvings produced during this time strongly resemble Soviet art. 8" to 9.5" tall. $200-250.

This pair of carvings shows farmers sowing their fields. 5.5" tall. $125-175.

With mountains nearby, skiing is a popular pastime in and around northern Italy and this carving of a skier is one of several skiing models produced by the ANRI carvers during the first half of the 20th century. Female figures on skis were also made. $150-175.

This very old carving depicts a young shepherd with a lamb and was produced in the early 1920s. $135-150.

Most vintage ANRI items can be categorized as either realistic or caricature carving. Most of the figurines shown to this point have been realistic. This little guy on skis is what is called a caricature carving meaning his features are exaggerated and cartoonish. This figure is only 3" tall and was made in the 1920s. Dogs on skis were also produced. $30-45.

Another man on skis, this one is 4.5" tall. $30-45.

Carved busts or portrait carvings are scarce but don't seem to inspire the same level of interest as ANRI figurines and other items. 3.5" tall. $55-85.

These photos illustrate the many faces, poses, and sizes of ANRI caricature carvings. They range in size from 2" to 7" tall. $30-65.

The two caricature carvings in this photograph are older and skillfully carved. $45-70.

A well-rounded collection of ANRI carvings should have at least a few of these comical characters to illustrate the diversity of the talent among ANRI carvers. $30-65.

These three carvings were Cristi creations made of special hardwoods and issued during the 1950s in a series of sixteen or more models with both men and women. From 5" to 7" tall, they were incorporated into other items such as the desk pieces seen in a previous chapter of this book. Sports figures included: golf, skiing, hunting, hiking, and bowling. Some of the professions depicted were lawyers, shoemakers, teachers, yachtsmen, and sea captains. $55-85.

These figures were from a series of thirty-five figures issued during the 1950s. ANRI catalogs state that they are made of fine hardwoods and were available in two sizes, 7" and 10" tall. The figures in this series were also given titles but collectors should be aware that the titles changed from one trade catalog to another. As titled in one catalog, they are, from the left: "Latest News," "Tidbits," "Good Sport," "A Good Price," and "A Fine Specimen." $65-95.

Here are four more from the series of thirty-five 1950s figures: "Keep Sleeping," "Off To Feast," (one painted), and "Duet." $65-95.

Another series issued during the 1950s portrayed men and women involved in sports activities. Included were tennis, bowling, skiing, and golf. $65-100.

The Artist is a unique ANRI carving which depicts a man wearing bifocal glasses posed before a painting in progress. There is an actual canvas on the easel in front of him. The base of the piece is 5.5" by 3.5", the figure is 5.75" tall, and overall it is 7 5/8" tall to the top of the easel. This model was introduced in the 1950s. $150-175.

A completely different type of artist is this comical figure that was designed by G. Sestini. 6.75" tall, 3" wide, 2 3/8" deep. $70-85.

The Alpine children, seen on ANRI napkin rings, bottle stoppers, and other items, were also sold as single figurines. Be aware that they were not produced and sold exclusively by ANRI and may be indistinguishable from those produced by other companies. 2.5" to 4" tall. $20-40.

ANRI gnomes were carved in some of the same poses seen in their larger realistic or caricature figurines. These are less than 3" tall. $30-45.

Pictured here are a group of ANRI smokers. They are characterized by a metal tube inserted into a hole in their mouths. Tiny "cigarettes" were sold that fit into the tubes and when lit, they produced a semi-realistic illusion that the figures were smoking. They are 2.5" tall and quite uncommon. $45-65.

These tiny little figures are less than 3" tall and were produced before the 1950s. Many, many models in this size and style were made. $45-70.

The very tiny carvings ANRI produced during the first half of the 20th century represent some of their most creative work, and in many cases, due to the skill required, are more valuable than similar ones in larger sizes. The figurines shown here are 1.5" to 3.5" tall. $50-75.

The average collector might not be aware that these little figures, in their fine fabric native costumes, were produced by ANRI and pictured in trade catalogs as early as 1912. Dozens of different figures of this type were added to pincushions and trinket boxes and it is amazing that these have been found in the pristine condition shown here. This trio still has original ANRI labels. $200-250.

Music has always been an integral part of the history and heritage of the Tyrol region and ANRI has produced carvings of musicians for almost 100 years. Figurines depicting men and women with concertinas or accordions, stringed instruments, horns, and drums are shown in ANRI trade catalogs from the time of the company's founding.

Vintage figurine collectors may also discover, with persistent searching, that they can assemble a matching set of similar musicians to form a band or orchestra. Some matched sets were produced but the figures were sold separately.

The most common musicians produced by ANRI were those playing concertinas. This less common man is seen seated, serenading his dog. $125.

When seen in a large group, the variations from one concertina-playing musician to another are awe-inspiring. The figures shown range in height from 3" to 9" and were made from the early 1920s until the mid-1950s. $35-100.

The very unusual figure in the center is playing a harmonica. 7.25" tall. $75-95.

Musicians with guitars are another common ANRI carving. These range from 3" to 8" tall and were made from the mid-1920s until the early 1950s. $35-100.

The mandolin is an instrument similar to the guitar, with an oval shaped body. These mandolin players vary in height from 5.25" to 8.5" tall. It's interesting to note that few women musicians are seen but those found are most often carved playing a mandolin. $55-120.

This trio of mandolin players ranges in size from 5.5" to 8" tall. The man with the umbrella is mounted on a music box that is original to the piece and was produced in the mid-1920s. Mandolin player on music box, $250.

Another stringed instrument often found is the standing bass fiddle. These three are 3.5" to 7.5" tall. $45-100.

The tallest of this group is 7.5" tall and the smallest is 4" tall. $40-100.

These violinists range in size from 2.5" to 8" tall. $40-100.

ANRI drummers are often playing colorful red and green drums. These models range from 5" to 8" in height. $65-120.

The ANRI brass section is a varied lot with musicians playing everything from trumpets to tubas. These figures range from 4.5" to 7.25" tall. $45-120.

The small, unpainted horn player is one of a matching series of musicians, 4.25" tall. $35-55.

Figurines, like this model, with a pair of musicians playing a guitar and a concertina were made as early as 1912. The larger of the two shown is 10" tall by 7" wide and the smaller is 7" tall by 4.25" wide. $150-200.

This beautiful series consisted of ten musicians on atypical black round bases. These musicians were produced before 1920. It was last pictured in an ANRI trade catalog in 1921. Missing from this collection are the conductor, and the clarinet, piccolo, and trumpet players. 5.5" tall. $200-250.

This series of musicians on more traditional bases was carved before the end of World War One when Santa Cristina/Val Gardena was still part of Austria. They are 7" to 7.5" tall. Similar figures were produced through the late 1940s and during the early to mid-1950s. $135-160.

ANRI made caricature carvings with musical instruments but most are very small. These range from 1.75" to 5" tall. $35-65.

Gnomes were also carved playing a variety of instruments. Shown, 3" to 5" tall. $40-65.

As you search for musicians for your own collection, it is important to remember that you are competing with collectors who may actually play the flute, guitar, tuba, violin, or other instrument. This adds a bit of a challenge to the search. These figurines are 2.5" to 5.25" tall.

The tiniest of the musicians ANRI produced were less than 2" tall. Their value is consistent with larger carvings because of the skill required, and because fewer were made in this size. $55-80.

From its inception, ANRI produced literally thousands of religious items. Figures of Christ, Madonnas, saints, angels, and monks were made in countless numbers, as well as a variety of nativity sets. Only a few are pictured here because it would require several volumes of books this size to adequately present just this category.

This monk with a violin and music stand is 8.5" tall and was produced in the 1950s. A similar 14.5" figurine was pictured in ANRI trade catalogs from 1925. $125.

This group illustrates only a few of the different Monks ANRI produced. The 5" figure on the left with snuffbox in hand is from the 1920s. The second monk, also with a snuffbox, is from the middle to late 1940s and is 8" tall. The unusual unpainted monk is 6.5" tall and the small one on the right is from a set of six in various poses, 3.5" tall. $75-150.

These monks, from a series of twelve, were not carved of wood but formed from a material called Sculptulite then mounted on polished wood bases. Hundreds of items were made of this material and carry the TORIART label, a registered trademark of the ANRI Company. 4.5" to 5.5" tall. $65-95.

Statues of St. Francis of Assisi are easily found and ANRI produced figurines of many, many other saints, as well. The unpainted figure on the left was carved as a prototype but never produced for the general public. 11.5" tall. $500. The smaller conventional St. Francis figurine is 6.5" tall. $45-75.

These two figures do not appear in any ANRI trade catalog. The ANRI research team could find no records for their production indicating that they were either commissioned figures or were not produced in large numbers for retail sales. The figure on the left represents Moses and the one on the right is a Jesuit Priest, 8" tall. $175-200.

Religious carvings in bas-relief were produced in literally hundreds of models. This pair is 6" diameter and depicts Jesus and the Virgin Mary. $40-50.

ANRI Doctors

Collectors of ANRI doctor figurines have their work cut out for them. There were actually several different sets produced and doctor figurines were also included in other series. At least four different types of doctor figures were produced. Two were made completely of wood while two others were created either partially or completely of the composite material called Sculptulite under the TORIART label.

These two figures are from the Sestini series. The bodies and bases are carved wood with heads made of Sculptulite. They are the orthopedist and nurse from a set of fourteen that also included a gynecologist, pediatrician, psychiatrist, general practitioner, surgeon, optometrist, ear, nose and throat specialist, dentist, radiologist, pharmacist, veterinarian, and chemist. This is the only nurse ANRI produced. $75-115.

It can be difficult to differentiate between them but the following photographs should prove helpful. The doctor on the left is a Mahlknecht design made of wood. The center figure is by Cristi and is part of a set of nineteen figures representing different professional and sports figures. Cristi figures are carved of fine hardwoods and about 7" tall. The doctor on the right was created by Guilio Sestini.

This group of doctors is from a set of twelve that ANRI trade catalogs advertise simply as caricatures and are the radiologist, veterinarian, surgeon, chemist, pharmacist, general practitioner, oculist, two additional GPs, and the dentist. $75-100.

The nine doctors in this photograph are from a series of twelve made completely of Sculptulite under the TORIART label. They are, from the left: general practitioner, surgeon, pharmacist, gynecologist, orthopedist, dentist, ear, nose and throat specialist, oculist, and radiologist. The complete set also included a veterinarian, psychiatrist, and pediatrician. Each is about 5.5" tall. $75-100.

Charles Dickens Figures

In the early 1920s, ANRI introduced a series of twelve carvings depicting characters from novels by Charles Dickens. The original set shown in ANRI catalogs from 1925 was 9" tall and included: Mr. Pickwick, Dolly Varden, Mr. Pecksniff, Sarah (Sairy or Mrs.) Gamp, the Artful Dodger, Mr. Dick, Jacob (Job.) Trotter, Sam Weller, Little Nell, Joe the Fat Boy, David Copperfield, and Mr. Micawber. In 1926 ANRI added figures in two additional sizes, 3.25" and 5.25" tall.

It was during the mid-1920s that the Dickens characters were also used on bottle stoppers. This series of both figurines and stoppers have the characters' names painted on them, usually on the base of the figurines, and on bottle stoppers, either on the wooden bases or the back of the figures themselves.

It is interesting to note that at some point the figure of Captain Cuttle was added and may be found as both a figurine and bottle stopper. To date, no bottle stopper of Little Nell has been discovered.

The figure of Mr. Dick is shown here in each of the three sizes, 9", 5.25" and 3.25" tall. Sizes for all figures are approximate, varying slightly from one to another and there are striking differences in the same characters from one carving to the next.

Sam Weller and Sarah Gamp, which is spelled 'Sari' on this figurine but is usually labeled "Mrs. Gamp" or "Sairy Gamp." 9" and 5.25".

These four figures of the Artful Dodger illustrate the differences in carvings through the years. The smaller is 5.5" and the other three are 9" tall.

The two carvings on the left are Mr. Pickwick and the three on the right are David Copperfield.

There are a couple of interesting errors on two of the three figurines seen here. On the left, a carving, which is obviously David Copperfield, is labeled Joe the Fat Boy. Sam Weller, the center figure, was painted with his last name spelled "Waller." The figure on the right is Mr. Pecksniff. Each of these figures is 9" tall. Dickens Characters, 9" tall, $350-400.

All the figurines shown here are approximately 5" to 5.5" tall. From the left: Dolly Varden, Mr. Dick Mrs. Gamp, (whose name was mistakenly painte as Mr. Gamp) David Copperfiel Job. Trotter, Joe the Fat Boy, Capt Cuttle, and Sam Weller (also with the misspelling as Waller). Dickens Characters, 5" series, $250-300.

These characters are, from the left: Little Nell, Job. Trotter, Capt. Cuttle, Mr. Pecksniff, Mr. Micawber, and Dolly Varden. Dickens Characters, 3.25" series, $175-200.

These are als 3.25" figurine and are, from the left: Sam Weller, (two figures) Artf Dodger, (two figures) Capt Cuttle, Davi Copperfield (two figures) Mr. Dick, Dolly Varden Joe the Fat Boy, Mr. Pickwick, an Mr. Micawbe $175-200.

ANRI Animal Figures

The wonderful world of ANRI animal figurines is as varied by species as a walk through a zoo. The greatest numbers of carvings of animals produced since the beginning of the ANRI Company were dogs, but cats, squirrels, bears, horses, deer, and even elephants were made.

ANRI had fun with animals, too, carving them doing human things as you'll see. The most common dog breeds seen are terriers including, Scottish, Skye, and wire-haired fox, but there were also St. Bernard's, Pekinese, English bulldogs, Spaniels, and more.

Animal families, an adult dog, cat, or other animal with two smaller ones connected by delicate chains, were made from the early 1920s until the late 1950s or mid-1960s. Shown here are a family of Skye terriers and a hard to find family of cats. Adult animals range from 2" to 3.5" with the offspring carved as small as a half inch. $35-45.

Two family sets and a trio of single figures. The largest is less than 2" long. $20-40.

Dogs doing human things make for some interesting carvings like this dog on ice skates with a hockey stick. 3" long. $40-55.

Gordon or Springer Spaniels are a beautiful breed seen here as a family set and on ice skates playing hockey. $40-55.

We may not be sure of the breed, but we are sure that this pup has picked up a bad habit, probably from its owner. Wonder if he asks to go out to smoke, too? 4" long, $45-60.

Cute dogs, but these resemble what are commonly called "mutts" or mixed breeds. 3" to 4" long. $35-60.

Some of the ANRI dogs have made skiing their sport of choice while others are content doing normal doggie type things. $35-60.

The Saint Bernard is not just a pet in the mountainous regions of the Tyrol. They are famous for finding people who have become lost in the snow. ANRI paid tribute to these canine heroes in numerous carvings. $40-100.

These Pekinese pups range in size from less than 2" to over 3" long. $35-50.

Collectors of bottle stoppers and bar sets may recognize the cat in the first photograph. Similar figures were used atop bottle stoppers and as the handles for bottle openers and corkscrews. The dogs are over 3" long. $45-60.

Top & center: ANRI canines come in all sizes and breeds and all are charming. Some people collect one particular breed of dog in any form, therefore many ANRI pieces are in exclusive collections of that kind, like the Skye and Scottish terriers. Sometimes the competition will be fierce so ANRI collectors should be prepared to do friendly battle for their acquisitions.

One of the most enchanting sets of animals ANRI produced was the dog band. Like the Gröden musicians, pups may be found with a concertina, drum, horn, or stringed instrument. You may even find a conductor like the one seen here. Dog musicians were carved in several sizes from 2" to 4" tall. During the 1920s, ANRI also produced a set of musicians featuring Bonzo, a cartoon dog from that era. Dog musicians, \$45-65. Bonzo musicians, \$135-160.

As you can see, dog musicians vary from breed to breed and even from piece to piece, but a conscientious collector can complete a band with patience and persistence. This group is 2" to 2.75" tall. It is important to note that almost exact copies of the ANRI dog musicians are being produced at this time, but not by ANRI. A reproduction band is shown in Part Five of this book. Each, $45-65.

Much more difficult to find are ANRI bands with cats since fewer of the feline musicians were made. A sextet with conductor is pictured here. ANRI also produced an entire set of twelve Krazy Kat musicians in the 1920s. Cat musicians, $55-70. Krazy Kat musicians, $140-165.

ANRI carvers also made figurines of woodland creatures like the fox squirrels shown here. Similar carvings may be found on bottles stoppers, on corkscrews, and as decorative pieces on many other items. 2" to 4" tall. $25-35.

Bears are less common although many were produced. Most have found homes in collections dedicated exclusively to bears. Several models of Polar bears were also made. Shown from 2" to 4" tall. $55-75.

Few collectors are aware of the less common animals produced by the carvers of ANRI. The tiny elephant shown is a good example but there were also goats, pigs, camels, donkeys, cows, sheep, beavers, etc. $35-75.

In 1935, ANRI produced a set of tiny dogs made of Cembra pine to which small metal hanger loops were attached. The set consisted of twelve dogs, two each of six different breeds, and they were sold by sets. Production continued until about 1950. In the late 1990s a supply of them was found and sold through collectors' publications. At that time, boxes containing a gross could be bought for a few dollars. Lately, these tiny carvings have been popping up on Internet auction sites. $1-2.

These comical, stylized horses were pictured in ANRI trade catalogs as early as the mid-1920s. 2" to 4" tall. $110-125.

Other, more realistic carvings featuring horses and riders were also produced like this one showing a rider going over a jump. The figure shown was produced in the mid-1950s and has the ANRI green and gold foil pine tree label. At least seven models were made in this series with and without riders, or handlers. 5.5" and 7" tall. $150-175.

Just for fun, and to illustrate the wonderful imagination and skill of the ANRI carvers, here is a collection of items featuring the popular Skye terrier. Enjoy!

Part Five

ANRI Objets d'art etcetera

Even with the best efforts there is simply no way to cover the thousands of things ANRI produced during the "vintage" years. To do so would require a series of books similar to an encyclopedia, but we'll leave that project for another day.

There are a few ANRI items in Chapter Five that for all their beauty, quality, and function, just didn't fit into other categories, like music boxes, wall art, and chess sets. All ANRI objects are artfully done; many are truly works of art.

Before the late 1960s, ANRI produced music boxes that scarcely resemble those produced during the next four decades. These were made entirely of wood and incorporated figures and animals seen in many other applications during that time.

Music boxes were incorporated in bar sets and bar scenes, as seen in earlier chapters. Many figurines that were being sold individually were mounted on wooden bases containing musical inserts that played classical and traditional favorites.

In the 1950s and 1960s, ANRI produced an impressive collection of music boxes featuring busts of famous composers, each with a Swiss 38 note music box playing their well known compositions. These were made under the Toriart label and included Chopin, Verdi, Beethoven, Wagner, Brahms, Schubert, Bach, Tschaikovsky, Handel, Mendelssohn, Haydn, and Mozart.

It was also during the 1950s that ANRI began producing a series designed by G. Sestini called "ANRI Children." Production continued through the 1970s with new models and tunes added and retired each year.

Music boxes have always had a way of taking us back to a time or place. ANRI music boxes did that more beautifully than most.

This music box, with a boy and girl and a rabbit sitting under a pine tree, was produced in the late 1930s and is wound by twisting the top platform. The children and tree revolve as it plays. The base is 1.75" tall and 5" diameter; children figures are 3.25" tall and it is 9.5" tall overall. It is made completely out of wood and for all its charm and sweetness of subject, the tune it plays never fails to bring a chuckle, a beautiful rendition of "How Dry I Am." $100-150.

The figures atop these music boxes may look familiar if you are a collector of ANRI figurines. The goose girl figure is 5 3/8" tall on a base that is 2 3/8" square. The music box is just over 5" diameter and it plays "Edelweiss." The figurine of a couple reading a newspaper is 4.75" tall on a 3 5/8" by 2.25" base. The music box is 5.5 diameter and plays "Blue Danube Waltz." Both figures revolve as the music plays. $150-200.

How romantic! Two couples dance and twirl atop these music boxes from the late 1940s. On the left, the smaller couple is 4.75" tall, the base is 2.5" diameter, and the music box is 4" diameter. The taller couple is 7 5/8" tall and the music box is 4.75" diameter. Both couples revolve as the music plays. $165-220.

The Sestini designed music box on the left was produced in the mid-to-late 1950s. It is an early example of the "ANRI Children" produced in the 1970s with some parts made of Sculptulite, but the one shown was made entirely of wood. It is 6" tall, the base is 4.75" diameter, and it rotates as it plays "Edelweiss." Siegfried Hafner created the figures seen atop the music box on the right. The Hafner figurines, carried by ANRI during the mid-1960s, were stylized boys and girls in whimsical poses. During this period ANRI trade catalogs stated that "first quality, long-play, lateral-wound, 28-note Swiss Thorens movements" were used in all music boxes. The Hafner music box is 7.25" tall overall. The base is 4.25" by 3.5" and 2.25" tall. The children rotate as it plays "Try To Remember." $100-150.

There were many wonderful things produced by ANRI carvers, but some of the least well known, until now, were the bas-relief carvings, which are figures and scenes carved into wood. A skillful artist is able to create art that deceives the eyes into seeing great depth in relatively shallow pieces of wood.

ANRI relief carvings were produced as early as the 1920s with landscapes and scenes of life in the Tyrol. Music boxes with relief carved tops were produced for many years, as well as a series of collectors' plates for Christmas, and other special occasions.

Another form of wall art that came from the ANRI studios was the kitchen diorama. These dioramas were creations presenting miniature interior views of homes throughout the Alpine region.

This relief carving shows a local scene with a pine tree and barn in the foreground and mountains in the distance. ANRI carvings of this style were produced well into the mid-1960s. This one is 7.5" by 9" and retains the double ANRI sticker used from 1952-1954. $65-100.

These two plaques were products of a working relationship between the artists of Goebel, creators of the M. I. Hummel figurines, and the carving artists of ANRI. They measure 4" by 5.75" and the carvings are .75" thick. $65-85.

This bas-relief piece duplicates an original painting by Carl Spitzweg (1805-1885) represented in wood by Josef Malfertheiner. The ANRI carvers reproduced Malfertheiner creations during the 1960s and 1970s. "The Astronomer" was available in several sizes both painted and unfinished. 12" by 7". $300-400.

This Malfertheiner representation, "The Bookworm," is another from the art of Carl Spitzweg. It is unpainted and measures 7.5" by 5". Malfertheiner also created representations of famous artworks by Renoir, Brueghel, Defregger, Ankar, and others. $250-300.

Kitchen dioramas are folk art in the truest sense of the word. Carving skill and the clever use of miniature elements make them seem deeper than the 1" they actually are. ANRI produced dioramas in many sizes with varying degrees of detail. On the left, 4.75" x 3 3/8" and on the right, 5.5" by 4". $40-60.

This is one of the larger, more detailed dioramas. It has many of the same elements found in the small ones but so much more. Notice the miniature kitchen items, the guitar propped against the pantry shelves, and the hunting rifle hanging on the wall near the table. It also has working window shutters and the special addition of a built-in music box. The winding mechanism can be seen to the right of the open door. The music begins when the door is opened and stops when the door is closed. 17.5" by 10" and 2" deep. $65-85.

Here is another large kitchen diorama with three men playing cards and a woman bringing food to the table. The butter churn in the center foreground has a built in thermometer. 16" by 10.25" and 2.5" deep to the door. $65-85.

ANRI chess pieces were pictured in trade catalogs as early as the 1920s and chess sets are still being produced today. Early pieces were traditional, highly detailed figural carvings with realistic Kings, Queens, and Knights atop rearing horses.

Over the years ANRI has produced chess sets representing famous historic or literary characters, with pieces following those themes. Character sets include D'Artagnan, Nefertiti, King Arthur, King Richard, Camelot, and Monsalvat, to name only a few. During the1950s, a futuristic chess set was produced that ANRI called "Universum," the Space Age set, and the simple wooden pieces still look modern today. In the mid-1960s a Wild West set was produced with cowboys and Indians in opposing positions.

While chess pieces were sold together, often in beautiful fitted boxes, most chessboards were sold separately. It was once possible to purchase a complete set of thirty-two pieces for less than $100 but present day sets retail for several thousand dollars and are sold in fine gift shops all over the world.

The Monsalvat set has remained very much as seen here throughout its production. The Kings are 6" tall, Queens are 5.75" tall, and the Knights stand 5 1/8" tall.

When seen inside the custom fitted Mahogany box, it is easy to appreciate the beauty and quality of this ANRI chess set. $2000-3000.

That's Not ANRI

In the search for ANRI items even the most experienced collector may buy some thing only to discover later that it's not an authentic ANRI creation. It has happened to all of us. If you love all kinds of woodcarvings and your collection isn't limited to ANRI exclusively, it's no tragedy. On the other hand, no one wants to make a costly mistake so lets look at some items that may be mistaken for ANRI.

This lovely little girl is well carved and beautifully painted, but she is not an ANRI figurine. She was probably created in the Tyrol region but with so many talented carvers it may never be known exactly from where she originated.

A large carved monk decanter with a glass bottle insert and a matching table lighter, were produced in Austria. The decanter is musical and plays when the figure is lifted. Collectors should come to recognize a tiny dot of red paint on the inside corner of each eye as the identifying mark for these and similar non-ANRI items.

This bottle stopper is one of a series by the same Austrian producer identified by the dot of red paint on the inside corner of each eye. These typically also have felt hats or caps.

A German carved figure with a corkscrew head.

Here is an item that has fooled even experienced collectors. It's called a "toddy set," a wooden figure with a corkscrew inserted into the head. The body separates in the middle and holds a set of small metal cups. Most toddy sets were made in Japan.

This cigarette box has elements similar to the man on a barrel cigarette box produced by ANRI, but while the base, barrel, and legs are made of wood, the head is made of a composite material.

Three German stoppers produced after WWII.

More post WWII German stoppers.

This novelty bottle stopper uses a wooden lever mechanism similar to that used by ANRI, but this one was probably made in Japan.

Right: A black bird stopper/pourer of unknown origin.

Left: A push puppet in a leather brimmed hat. Origin unknown.

This crumb tray resembles ANRI in carving style but the type of wood is not consistent with the maple or pine they most often used. The dog's head that serves as the handle has a place for a crumb brush between its jaws. This is probably another German carving.

Collectors should be especially wary of certain items currently being produced that are reproductions of vintage ANRI pieces. This dog band is a perfect example. Each figure seems to be an exact copy of the original until they are compared side by side, like the two Scottish terriers on the right. The ANRI carving is the bass fiddle playing Scottie on the left.

Another group of dogs that are ANRI knockoffs, dressed in baseball uniforms. They're cute and clever but they're not ANRI.

This little "Whatzit," a figure of a man seated with his arms resting on his chest, is definitely an ANRI carving but it presents a mystery. The piece of wood beneath him shaped like an upside-down top or spindle is inserted into a hole that goes completely through the figure from top to bottom. What is it? More than likely it is a "fantasy" piece, something put together from two disparate pieces long ago. The figure is 1.5" tall and 1.5" wide. The spindle is an additional 1.5" tall making the item 3" tall.

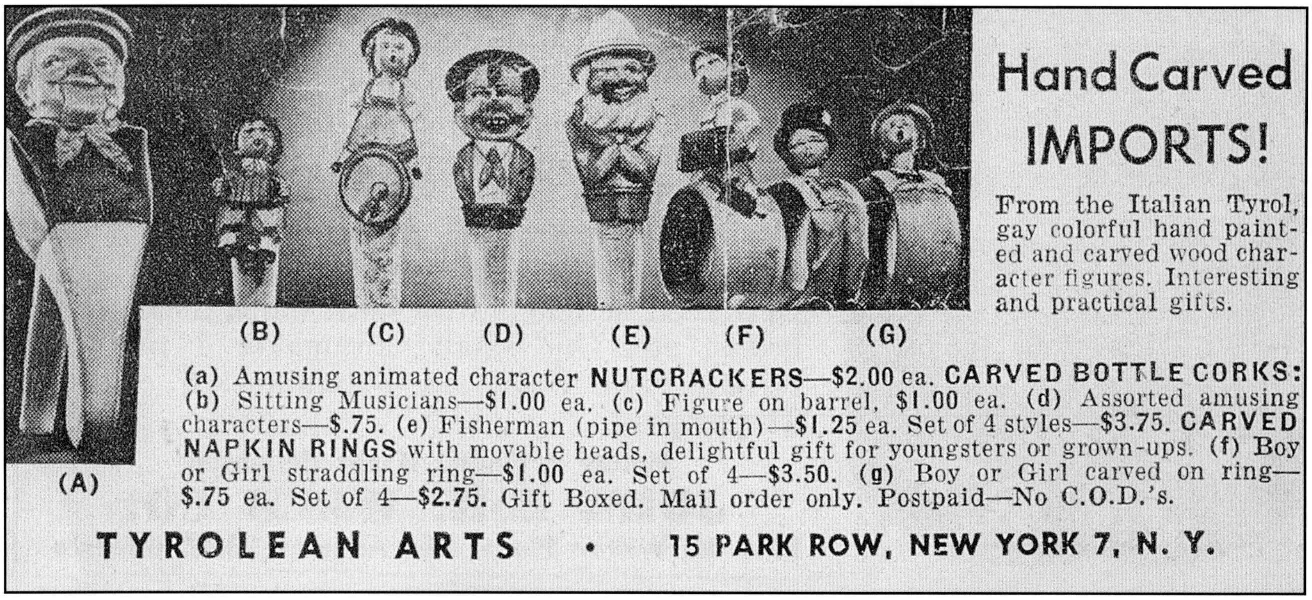

An advertisement from the November 1948 issue of *House Beautiful*.

FLASK AND BAR ACCESSORIES

Drinking Set. Genuine leather case containing four plastic cups. An ideal gift for travelers or vacationists. Can also be used as individual liquor cups.
14401J60
Suggested Retail $1.00

Plastic Flask with ribbed sides. Metal and chrome plated screw cap, nip cup attached. 12 ounce capacity, has novelty design painted on front for "Scotch," "Rye," and "Bourbon."
14402J110
Suggested Retail $1.75

Nip Cup Set: Made of genuine suntan top grain cowhide, contains three nested brass nickel plated cups. Closed by means of a strap over the cups, and a snap fastener. Size when closed: 2" x 1⅜".
14403J90 ....Suggested Retail $1.50

Packet Flask. Glass flask in genuine leather case. Exceptionally well made and finished. Snap button fastener. ½ pint.
14404J150
Suggested Retail $2.50

Pocket Flask. Glass flask in genuine leather case. Metal top which can be used for a cup. Snap button fastener. Will hold 12 oz.
14405J300
Suggested Retail $4.50

Hand carved, imported, figures on top of bottle stoppers with lever in back, which when pressed down, two faces come together and kiss. Size: 5" tall.
14406J115
Suggested Retail $1.75

Hand Carved Wood Bottle Stopper: Has two loving figures on top, manipulated by two levers.
14407J265
Sug. Retail $4.00

Imported bottle stopper with wooden hand carved figure of a dog. When pressing head back, it opens up spout so that liquid pours out of the mouth.
14408J175
Sug. Retail $2.75

Hip pocket flask, made of brass nickel plated, hammered outside, and tin-lined. Has a screw hinge top with a nip cup that screws on. Contents: 10 ounces. Size: 4 x 6½.
14409J375
Suggested Retail $5.50

Flask. 10 ounce slim glass flask with metal shoulder. Flask is encased in top grain cowhide leather case. Has metal cap and a screw on metal shot cup.
14410J450 ....Suggested Retail $7.50

Imported Cup Set: In tan color cowhide, hand sewn case. Contains four nickel nip one ounce cups, corkscrew and bottle opener and pouring cork. Size when closed: 3⅝" x 1½" circumference.
14411J450 ....Suggested Retail $7.50

Zipper Fastening Beverage Set made of genuine top grain cowhide with adjustable handle to carry in hand or over shoulder. Contains: two 12 oz. curved flasks. Each flask has a chrome finished screw cap and one chrome finished nip cup. Size when closed: 7¾x4½x3¼.
14412J1275
Suggested Retail $20.00

2 Pc. Flask Set in top grain ginger cowhide case with carrying handle, 6½x3¼x3¼. Tuck-tite lock with 8 oz. plastic flasks for Rye and Scotch with chromium top drinking caps.
14413J540 ....Suggested Retail $8.00

Flask Cocktail Set, top grain cowhide, 7½x6¾x4. Two 12 oz. flasks with chrome top drinking cup closures, plastic cocktail shaker with chrome top strainer cap and mixing spoon.
14414J1000 ....Suggested Retail $15.00

Zipper fastening beverage set, made of top grade ginger cowhide, with strong top handle for carrying. Contains three ½ pint flasks with nickel tops, each with a cowhide cover stamped "RYE", "SCOTCH", "BOURBON". Has four nickel cups, waterproofed lining. Size: 10 x 6 and ¾ x 2.
14415J1350 ....Suggested Retail $20.00

4 Pc. Bar Accessory Set, top grain cowhide, 9¼x4¼x1½". Zipper closing, ginger skiver lining, chrome plated fittings: 9" mixing spoon, olive fork, cocktail strainer and Bar King consisting of jigger cup, corkscrew and bottle opener.
14416J635 ....Suggested Retail $10.00

144 G. ED. TREBING COMPANY, CHICAGO 3, ILL.

A catalog page from the G. Ed. Trebing Company, Chicago, Illinois.